Scott Foresman - Addison Wesley

MATH

Homework Practice Workbook

Scott Foresman - Addison Wesley

Editorial Offices: Menlo Park, California • Glenview, Illinois
Sales Offices: Reading, Massachusetts • Atlanta, Georgia • Glenview, Illinois
Carrollton, Texas • Menlo Park, California

http://www.sf.aw.com

Overview

Practice Worksheets provide additional exercises for students who have not mastered key skills and concepts covered in the Student Edition. A Practice worksheet is provided for each core lesson of the Student Edition.

Lesson worksheets provide exercises similar to those in the Practice and Explore lessons of the Student Edition.

ISBN 0-201-36792-0

Printed in the United States of America

9 10 11 12 13 14 15 – VHG – 10 09 08 07 06 05

Contents

Chapter 9: Time and Money

Chapter 10: Explore Actions with Numbers

Chapter 11: Larger Numbers

Chapter 12: Explore Addition and Subtraction

Problem Solving:
Making Decisions

Directions Draw an X on each animal inside the fence. Circle each animal outside the fence. Draw an X on each thing inside the fish tank. Circle each thing outside the fish tank. **Notes for Home** Your child used the words *inside* and *outside* to decide the location of objects. *Home Activity:* Ask your child to name objects inside and outside a drawer.

Use with pages 11–12. **5**

Name _____

Naming Attributes

Directions In each row put an X on the one that is different. Tell how it is different and how the others are the same. **Notes for Home** Your child identified items by how they are the same and different. *Home Activity:* Ask your child to find two or more things, such as articles of clothing, that are the same in some way and tell you how they are the same.

Name _____

Same and Different Colors

Directions Circle the object in each row that does not belong. Color the objects that are the same with the same color. Color the object that does not belong a different color. **Notes for Home** Your child identified objects with the same color and objects with a different color. *Home Activity:* Ask your child to find objects, such as plates, with the same color and objects with a different color.

Name _____

Same and Different Shapes and Sizes

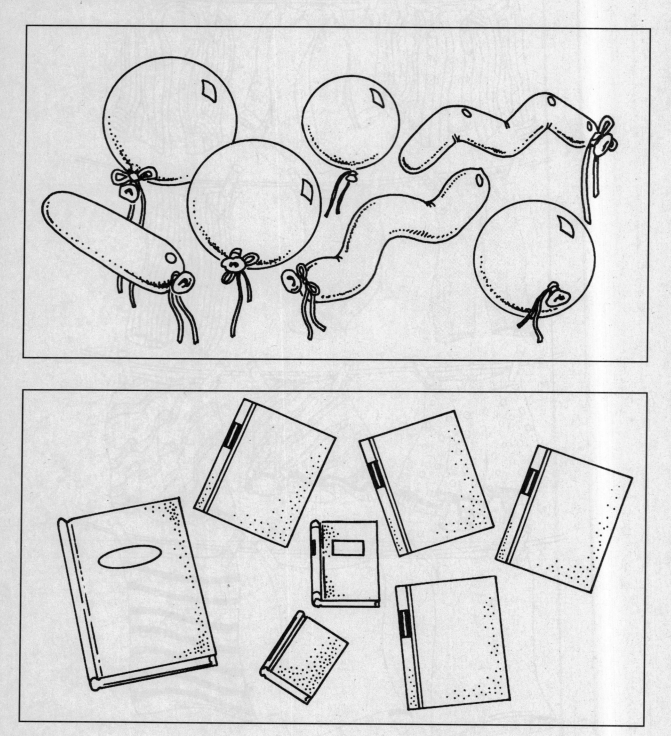

Directions In the first box, color the balloons that are the same shape. In the second box, color the books that are the same size. **Notes for Home** Your child identified objects with the same shape but different size, and objects with the same shape and size. *Home Activity:* Ask your child to find items of clothing with the same size and different shape, and items with the same shape and different size.

Name _____

Problem Solving:
Use Logical Reasoning

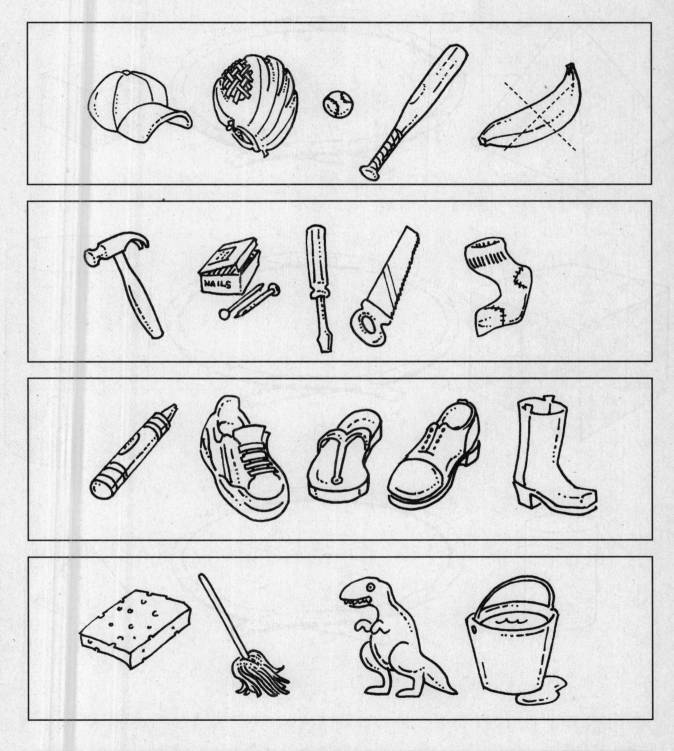

Directions In each box, draw an X on the object that does not belong. Tell why it does not belong. **Notes for Home** Your child used logical reasoning to decide which object in a group does not belong and explained why. *Home Activity:* Assemble groups of objects that are alike in some way, such as containers of food. Include an object that does not belong. Ask your child to tell what does not belong and explain why.

Sort

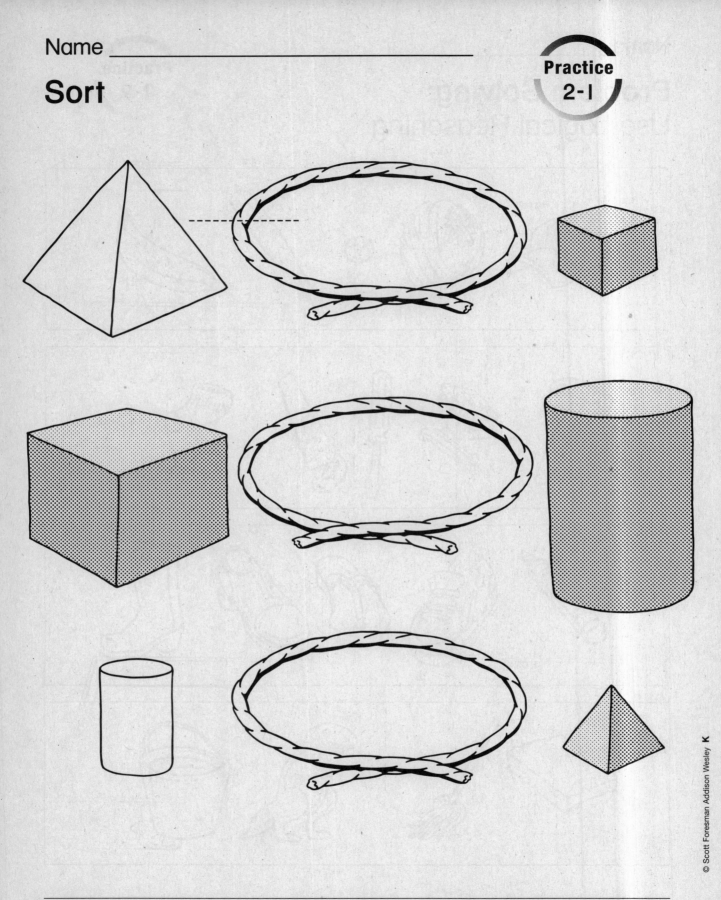

Directions Sort the blocks by shape. Draw a line from each block to show your sorting. **Notes for Home** Your child sorted objects into groups based on one attribute. *Home Activity:* Ask your child to sort shirts by color and socks by size.

Name _____

Sort and Resort Objects

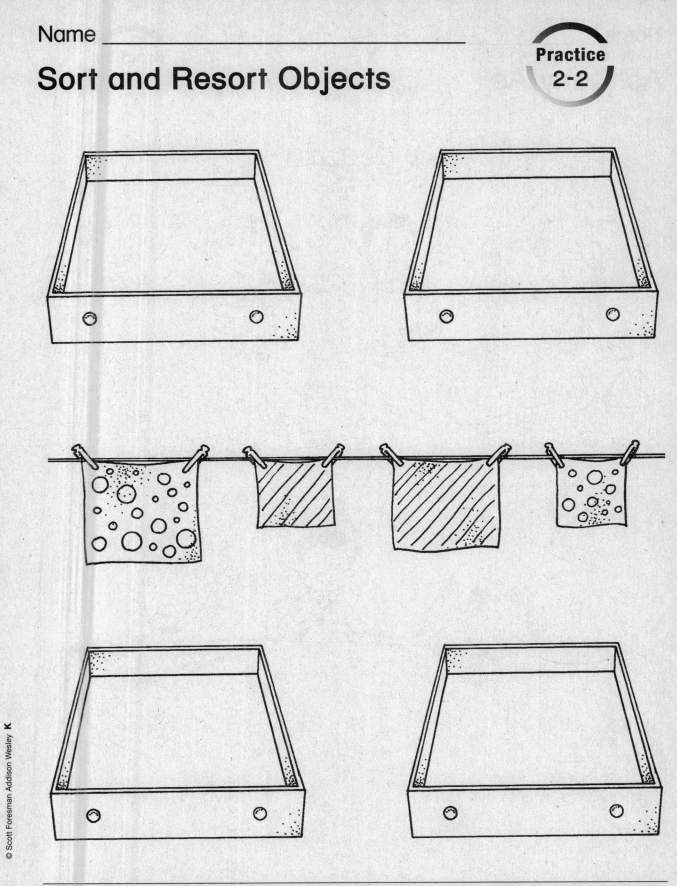

Directions Draw pictures to sort the scarves one way and then in a different way. **Notes for Home** Your child sorted objects by one attribute and then resorted the same objects by a different attribute. *Home Activity:* Ask your child to sort and resort some shirts.

Name _____

As Many As

Directions Draw one ball for each child at the beach. Draw one book for each child at the table. **Notes for Home** Your child drew objects to show a one-to-one match. *Home Activity:* Ask your child to match objects, such as shoes and socks, to make a one-to-one match.

More, Fewer

Directions Above the children, draw more hats than children. Below the children, draw fewer chairs than children.
Notes for Home Your child identified groups that have more and groups that have fewer objects than a given group. *Home Activity:* Ask your child to make a group of coins, then make a group that has more and a group that has fewer.

Name _____

Problem Solving:
Use Logical Reasoning

Directions Color the one that belongs with each group. **Notes for Home** Your child colored pictures to show the item that belongs with each group. *Home Activity:* Ask your child to sort socks by color.

Graphs

Are there more 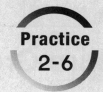 or ![shell] ?

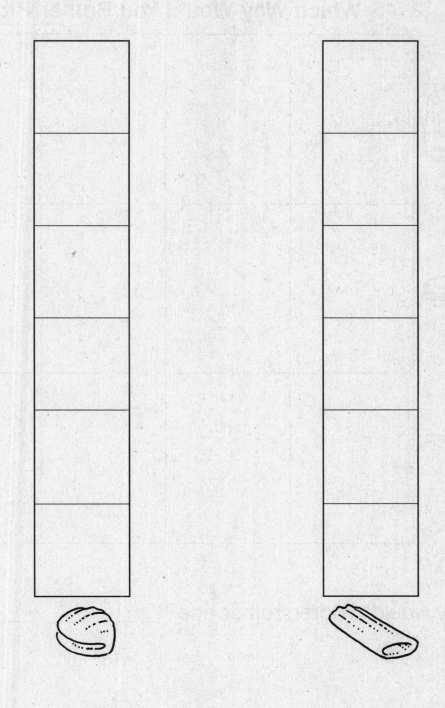

Directions Take a handful of pastas. Sort them to make a graph and compare the groups of objects. Are there more shells or zitis? **Notes for Home** Your child used objects to make a graph and compare the groups of objects. *Home Activity:* Ask your child to take a handful of two kinds of buttons or beans and make a graph to compare the groups.

Name _____

Picture Graphs

Which Way Would You Rather Ride?

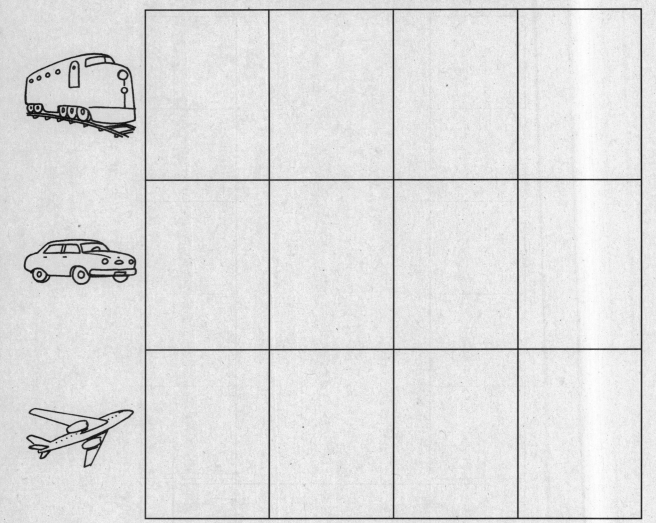

Which way would children rather ride? _____

Directions Find out from other children which way they would rather ride. Make a picture graph. Answer the question. **Notes for Home** Your child surveyed a group to find out which of three ways they would rather ride. *Home Activity:* Have your child ask family members and friends which way they would rather ride and draw pictures to make a graph. Discuss which way is the favorite.

Problem Solving: Use Data from a Graph

Which Animal Would You Rather See at the Zoo?

Directions Which is the favorite animal to see at the zoo? Circle its label. Which is the least favorite? Draw an X on its label. **Notes for Home** Your child used a picture graph to decide which wild animal is the favorite.
Home Activity: Have your child find out which wild animal is the favorite among family members.

Find a Pattern

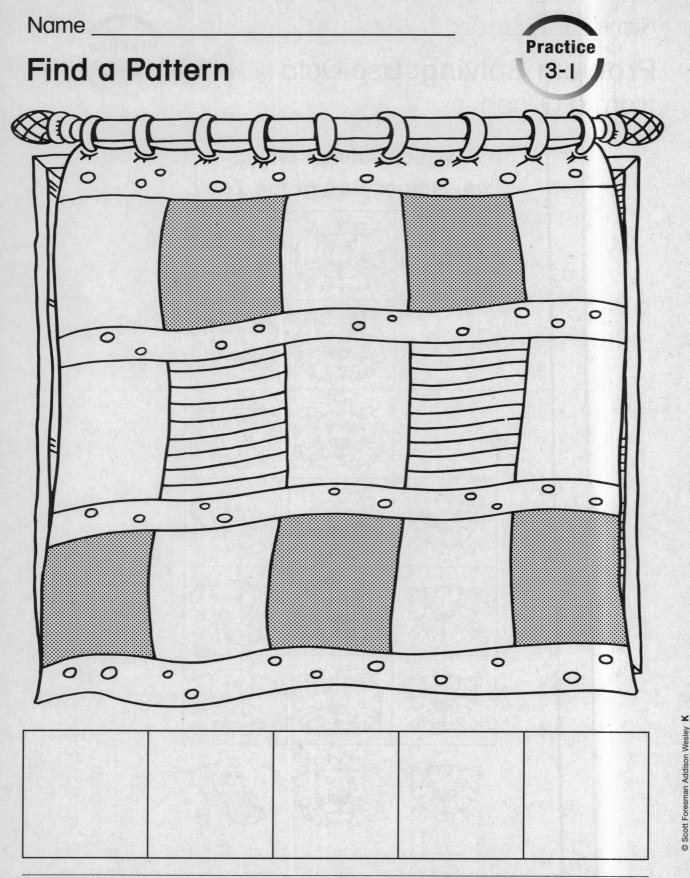

Directions Tell about the patterns you see on the curtain. Then choose one pattern on the curtain and show it at the bottom of the page. **Notes for Home** Your child recognized and described patterns, then copied a pattern. *Home Activity:* Make a two-color pattern using socks. Ask your child to describe the pattern.

Copy and Extend Patterns

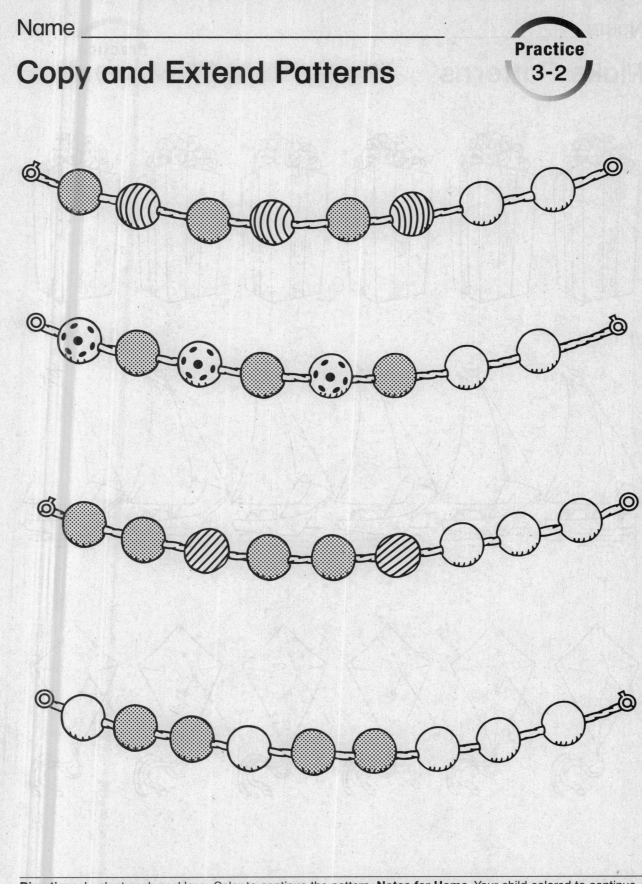

Directions Look at each necklace. Color to continue the pattern. **Notes for Home** Your child colored to continue patterns. *Home Activity:* Ask your child to copy one of the necklaces on the page and extend the pattern another 4 beads.

Make Patterns

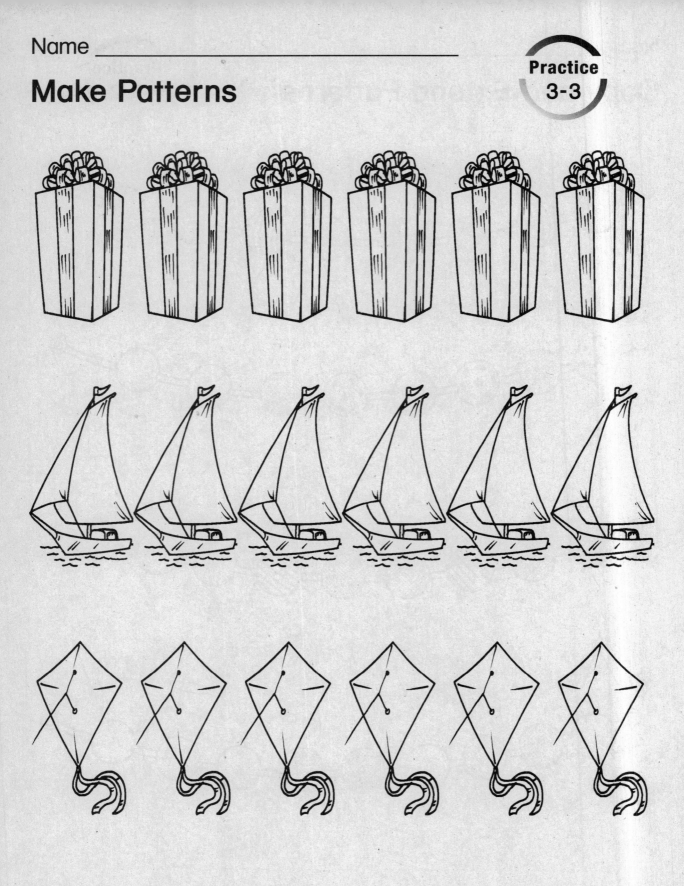

Directions Choose 2 colors to create a pattern in the first row. Then choose 3 colors to create your own patterns in the next 2 rows. Use 2 or 3 colors to create your own pattern. **Notes for Home** Your child created patterns with 2 or 3 colors. *Home Activity:* Give your child 3 books, 3 newspapers, and 3 magazines. Ask your child to make a pattern, using some or all of the items.

Name _____

Problem Solving:
Look for a Pattern

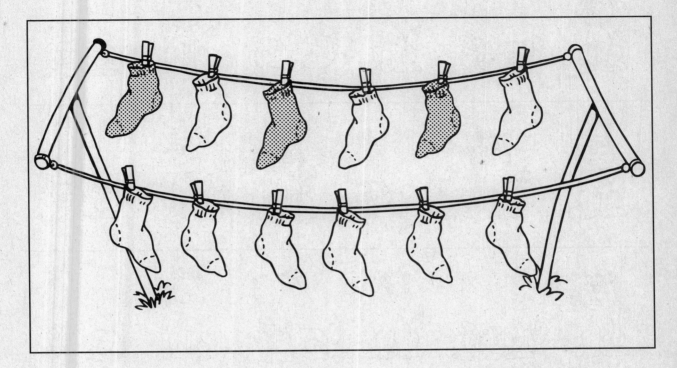

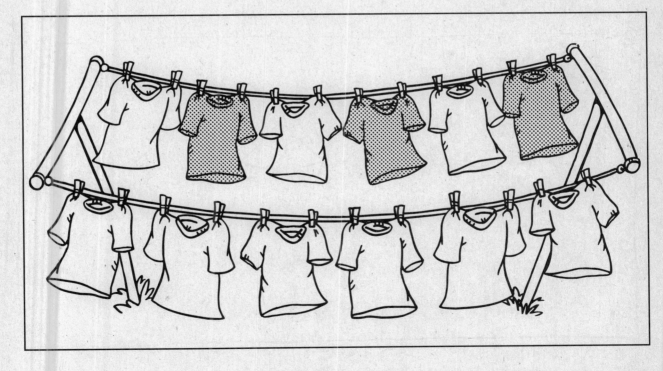

Directions Look at the top line of socks. What pattern do you see? Color to show that pattern on the other line of socks. Look at the T-shirts. What pattern do you see? Color to show that pattern on the other line of T-shirts.

Notes for Home Your child recognized and colored patterns. *Home Activity:* Have your child help you set the table for a family meal, and talk about the pattern he or she sees at the table.

Find Patterns That Are Alike

Directions Circle the 2 patterns that are the same. Draw a matching pattern. **Notes for Home** Your child decided which 2 patterns are alike and drew the same pattern. *Home Activity:* Help your child find matching patterns in clothing.

Name _____

Show Patterns in Different Ways

© Scott Foresman Addison Wesley **K**

Directions Find the pattern in each box. Then draw shapes to show it in a different way. **Notes for Home** Your child found AAB and AB patterns, and drew pictures to show each pattern another way. *Home Activity:* Ask your child to hop and jump to show an AB pattern. (hop, jump, hop, jump or jump, hop, jump, hop)

Name _____

Problem Solving:
Making Predictions

Directions Choose 2 colors. Color the pattern of stars and moons to show what part of the quilt is missing.
Notes for Home Your child predicted what elements of the patterns were missing and finished coloring the quilt.
Home Activity: Ask your child to talk about patterns, such as stripes, in clothing.

Name _____

Explore 1, 2, and 3

1

2

3

Directions Point to the number 1 and color the 1 turtle. Point to the number 2 and color the 2 lions. Point to the number 3 and color the 3 kangaroos. **Notes for Home** Your child read numbers and colored pictures to show 1, 2, and 3. *Home Activity:* Ask your child to point to number 3, number 1, and number 2.

Name _____

Count and Write 1 and 2

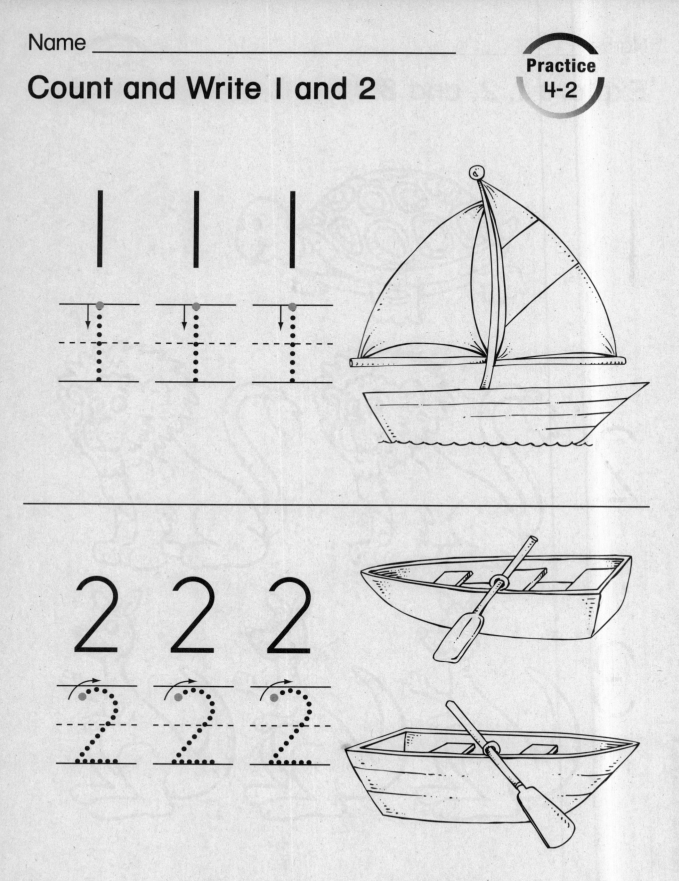

Directions How many sailboats do you count? Trace the number 1. How many rowboats do you count? Trace the number 2. **Notes for Home** Your child counted and wrote the numbers 1 and 2. *Home Activity:* Ask your child to trace over all the number 1s with a blue crayon and all the number 2s with a red crayon.

Name _____

Count and Write 3

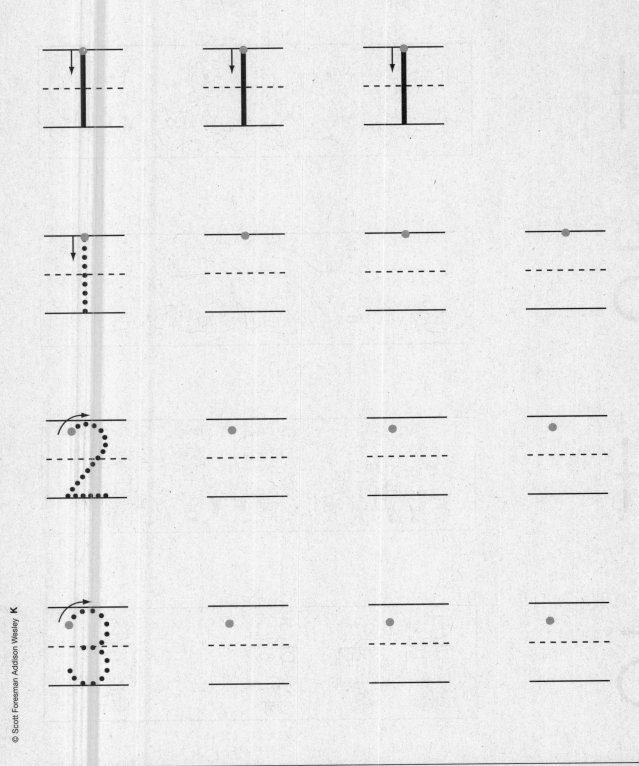

Directions Trace and write the numbers 1, 2 and 3. **Notes for Home** Your child traced and wrote the numbers 1, 2, and 3. *Home Activity:* Ask your child to draw a picture showing 3 dots.

Name _____

Explore 4 and 5

4 - - - - - - - - - - - -

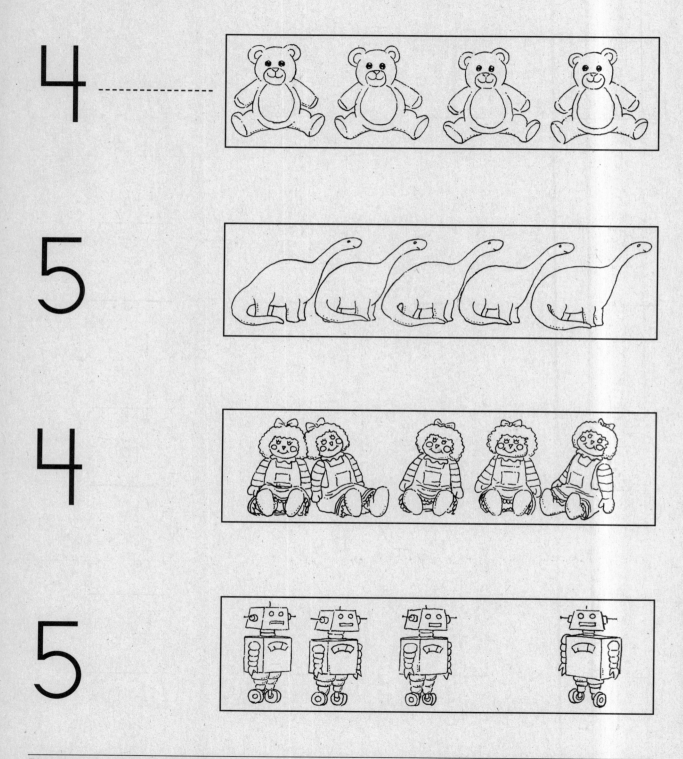

5

4

5

Directions Count the objects in each box. Then draw a line to match the number with the picture that shows how many. **Notes for Home** Your child matched groups of objects to numbers 4 and 5. *Home Activity:* Ask your child to show you a group of 5 objects.

Count and Write 4

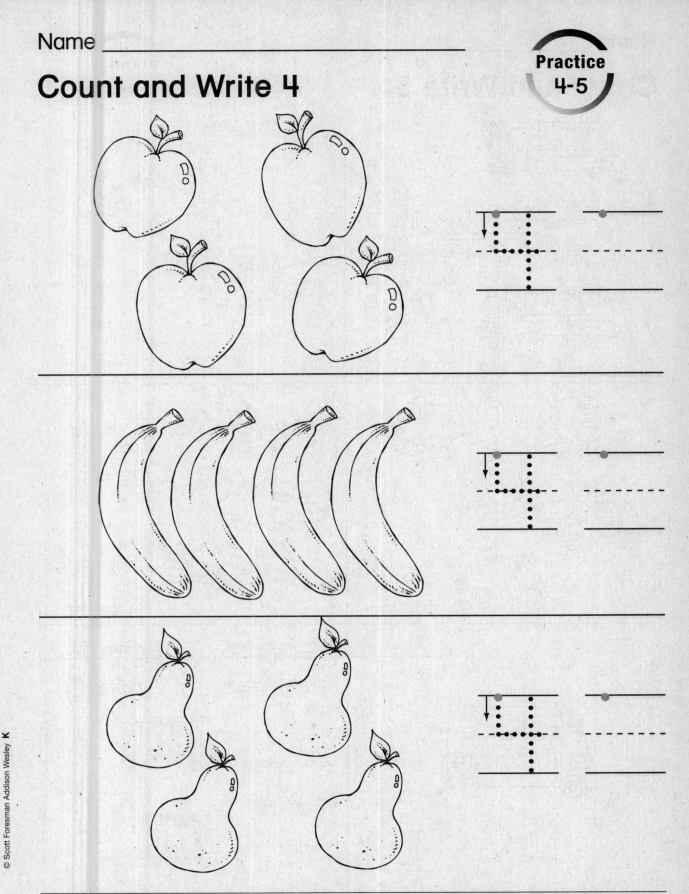

Directions Count the objects in each row. Trace and write how many. **Notes for Home** Your child counted groups of 4 objects and wrote the number 4. *Home Activity:* Ask your child to show you a group of 4 objects.

Count and Write 5

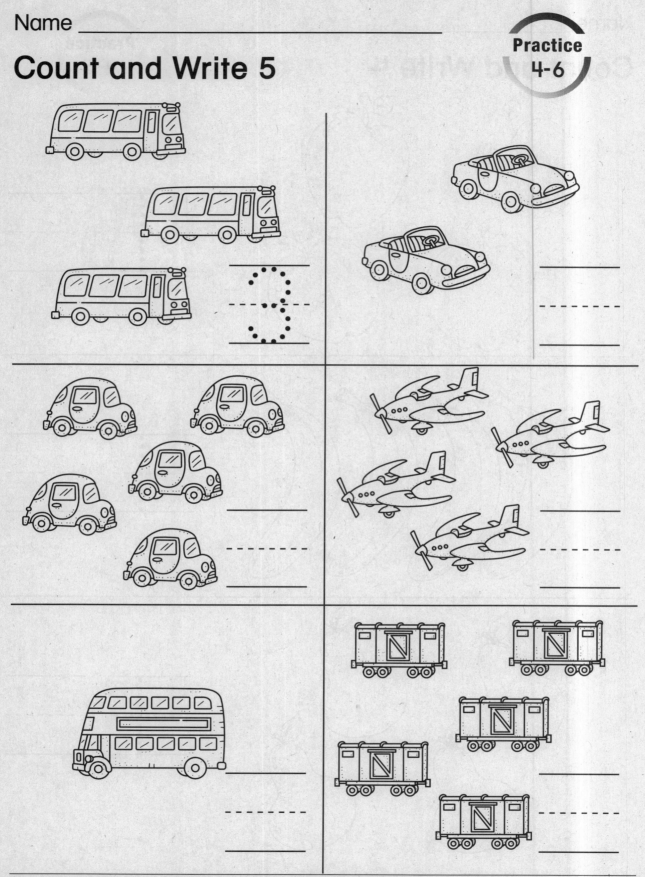

Directions Count the objects in each box. Write how many. **Notes for Home** Your child counted groups of 1 to 5 objects and wrote the numbers. *Home Activity:* Ask your child to point to the box that shows 5 objects; 3 objects; and 4 objects.

Explore and Write 0

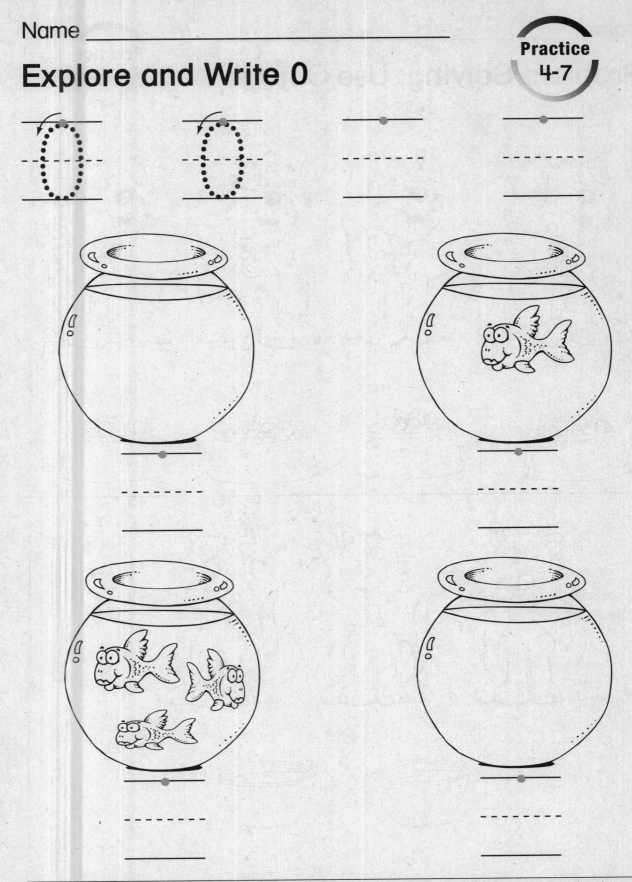

Directions Trace and write 0 at the top. Then circle the fish tanks that have no fish. Write 0 to show that there aren't any fish. **Notes for Home** Your child wrote the number 0. *Home Activity:* Ask your child to write the number 0.

Problem Solving: Use Objects

Directions Are there enough food dishes for each dog? (Yes) Use counters to find the answer. Are there enough water dishes for each cat? (No) Use counters. **Notes for Home** Your child solved problems using objects. *Home Activity:* Show your child a group of 3 pennies or small objects. Ask your child if there are enough pennies for 3 people to each have 1.

32 Use with pages 83–84.

Name _____

Sequence Groups of 1 to 5

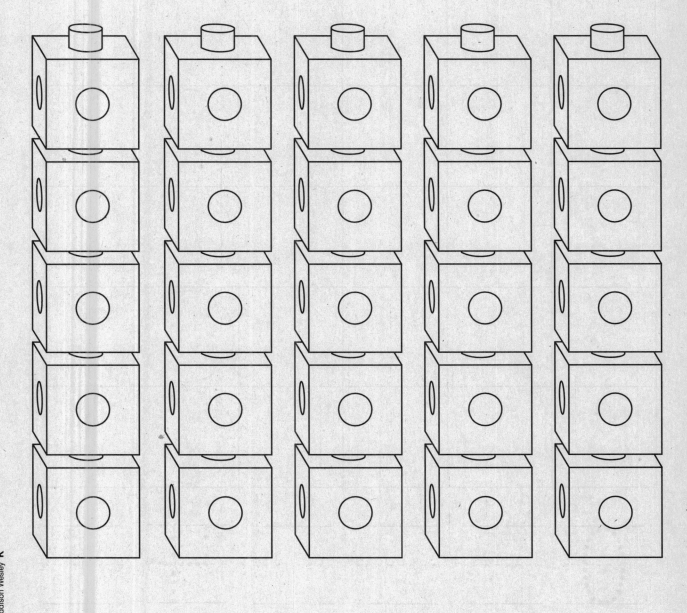

Directions Color the Snap Cubes to show numbers in order from 1 to 5. Tell how many of the Snap Cubes in each tower are colored. **Notes for Home** Your child colored Snap Cubes to show a sequence from 1 to 5. *Home Activity:* Ask your child to tell about the pattern he or she made by coloring. (Each tower increases by 1.)

Name _____

Order Numbers to 5

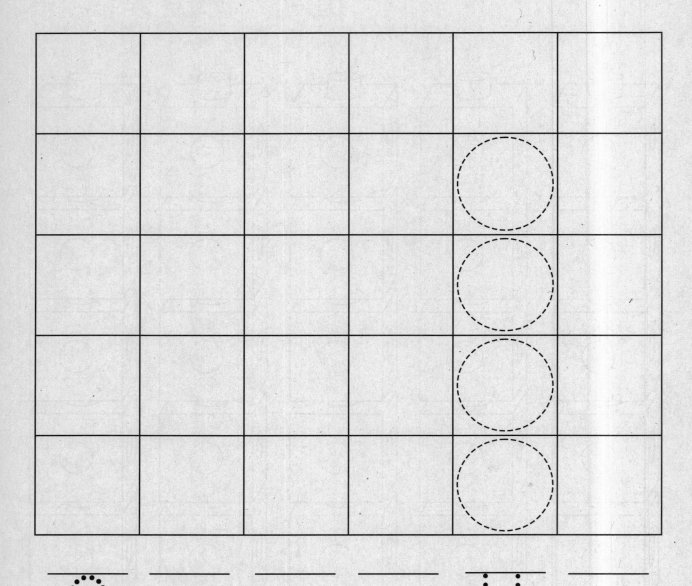

Directions Draw circles to show 0 to 5 in order. Then write the numbers. **Notes for Home** You child drew circles to show the numbers 0 to 5 and then wrote the numbers. *Home Activity:* Have your child count and write from 0 to 5.

Compare Numbers to 5

5   3

_____   _____

- - - - -   - - - - -

_____   _____

_____   _____

- - - - -   - - - - -

_____   _____

Directions Compare the groups of objects in each box. Write how many. Circle the groups in the top row with more. Color the groups in the bottom row with fewer. **Notes for Home** Your child compared groups of 1 to 5 objects and determined which group has more and which has fewer. *Home Activity:* Hold up two hands with a different number of fingers showing on each hand. Ask your child to tell you which hand shows more fingers and which shows fewer.

Name _____

Problem Solving: Draw a Picture

_ _ _ _ _ _ _

_ _ _ _ _ _ _

Directions Listen to the story. *4 friends are going on a picnic. Each friend wants an apple.* Draw a picture to show how many apples the friends need. Write the number. (4) Listen to another story. *5 friends are going to the beach. Each friend wants a pail.* Draw a picture to show how many sand pails the friends need. Write the number. (5)
Notes for Home Your child solved problems by drawing pictures. *Home Activity:* Ask your child to draw a picture to show how many apples are needed for each person in your family to have one.

Explore 6, 7, and 8

6

7

8

Directions Draw 5 blocks in each box. Then draw more blocks to show 6, 7, and 8. **Notes for Home** Your child drew 5 blocks in each box and then drew more blocks to show 6, 7, or 8. *Home Activity:* Ask your child to count and make groups of cans that are 1, 2, or 3 more than 5.

Name _____

Count and Write 6

Directions Count the pumpkins in the top row. Trace and write the number 6. Draw 6 boats in the next row. Write the number 6. Draw 6 suns in the next row. Write the number 6. Draw 6 balls in the bottom row. Write the number 6.
Notes for Home Your child practiced writing 6, and then drew pictures of groups of 6. *Home Activity:* Ask your child to make a group of 6 spoons and write the number 6.

Explore 9 and 10

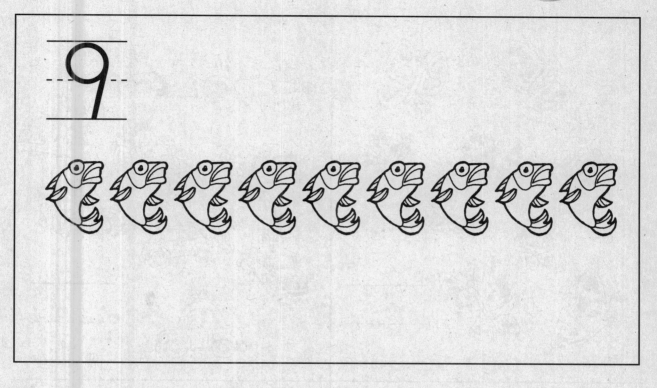

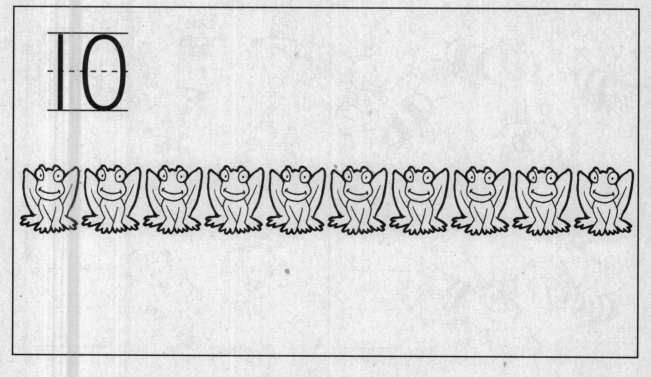

Directions Put a counter on each fish (frog). Move the counters to show another arrangement of the 9 fish (10 frogs). Draw the arrangement. **Notes for Home** Your child made arrangements of 9 and 10 counters. *Home Activity:* Ask your child to clap 9 times and then 10 times.

Count and Write 9

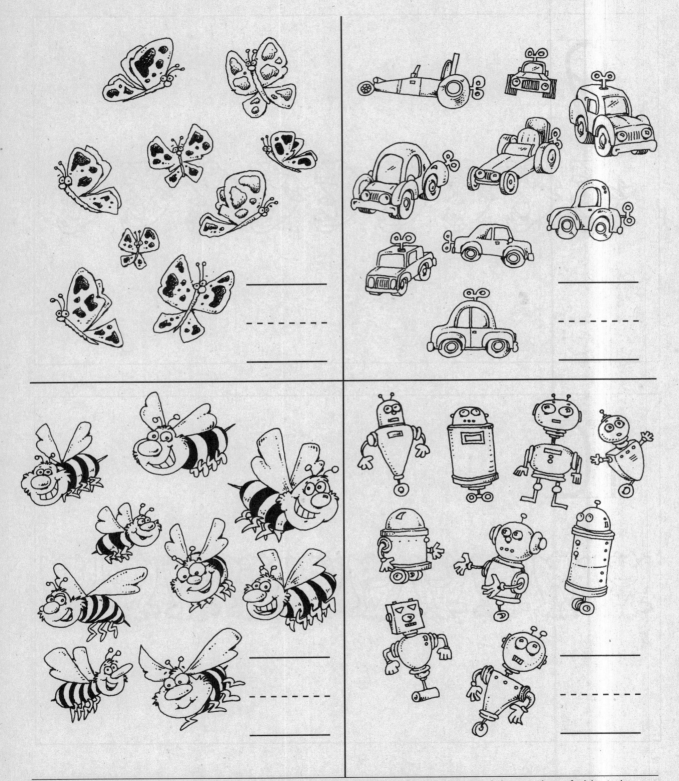

Directions Count how many. Write the number. **Notes for Home** Your child counted the number of objects in each box and wrote the number 9. *Home Activity:* Ask your child to hop or jump 9 times and write the number 9.

Name _____

Count and Write 10

_____   _____

- - - - - - - -   - - - - - - - -

_____   _____

              _____   _____

              - - - - - - - -   - - - - - - - -

              _____   _____

Directions Draw 10 stars around the spaceship. Then write the number 10. Draw 10 flowers in the garden. Then write the number 10. **Notes for Home** Your child drew groups of 10 and then practiced writing the number 10. *Home Activity:* Ask your child to count aloud to 10 and write the number 10.

Problem Solving: Use Data from a Picture

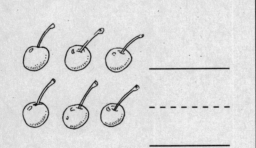

Directions Count the cherries. Write how many. Look for the fruit in the picture that is one fewer. Draw that fruit in the box on the right. Count the bananas. Look for the fruit in the picture that is one fewer. Draw that fruit in the box.
Notes for Home Your child counted the fruit and wrote the number to show how many. Then your child drew the group in the picture that has one fewer. *Home Activity:* Ask your child to count the pears in the picture. (4) Then ask your child to show a group of fruit that is one fewer than the pears. (bananas)

Sequence Groups of 10

5

6

7

8

9

10

Directions Count the number of marbles that are shaded. Color the remaining rows to show a sequence of groups to 10. **Notes for Home** Your child colored in marbles to show a sequence from 5 to 10. *Home Activity:* Ask your child to show you a group of 8 pennies, then 9 pennies, and 10 pennies.

Name _____

Order Numbers to 10

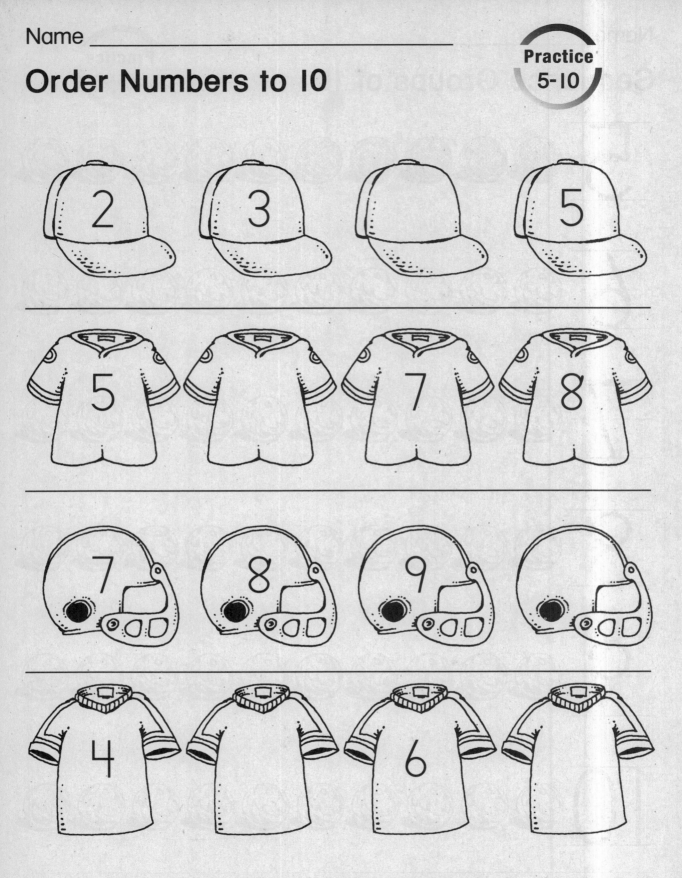

Row 1 (caps): 2 3 ☐ 5

Row 2 (jerseys): 5 ☐ 7 8

Row 3 (helmets): 7 8 9 ☐

Row 4 (shirts): 4 ☐ 6 ☐

Directions Write the missing number or numbers in each row. **Notes for Home** Your child wrote a missing number in a sequence of numbers. *Home Activity:* Write a number between 2 and 9 on a piece of paper. Ask your child to write the numbers that come one before and one after the number you selected, and to read all three numbers aloud.

Compare Numbers to 5 and 10

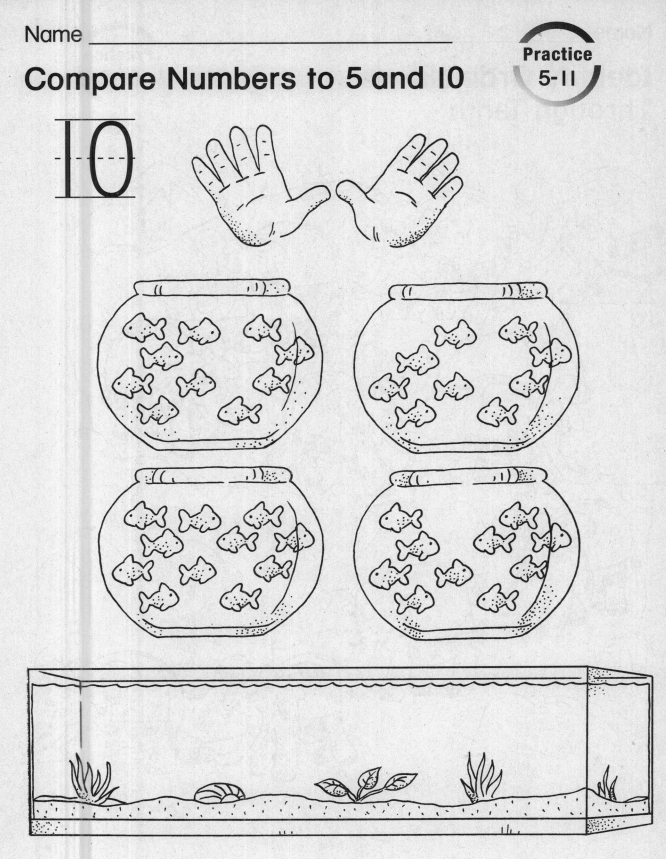

Directions Color groups fewer than 10 green. Color groups of 10 purple. Color groups more than 10 orange. Draw 10 fish in the aquarium. **Notes for Home** Your child found and colored groups fewer than 10 (green), groups of 10 (purple), and groups more than 10 (orange). Your child then drew 10 fish. *Home Activity:* Ask your child to count the fish he or she drew and then draw other fish to show more than 10.

Name _____

Identify Ordinals
Through Tenth

Directions Color the blanket on the first elephant blue. Color the blanket on the second elephant orange. Color the blanket on the third elephant green. **Notes for Home** Your child colored the blankets on the elephants according to their position in line. (first, second, and third) *Home Activity:* Ask your child to color the blanket on the fifth elephant red.

Name _____

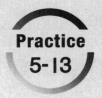

Problem Solving:
Guess and Check

Practice 5-13

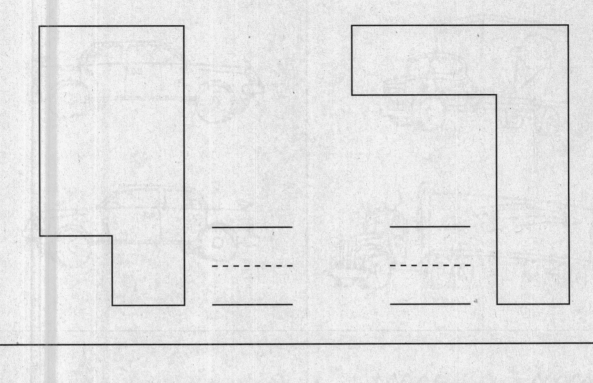

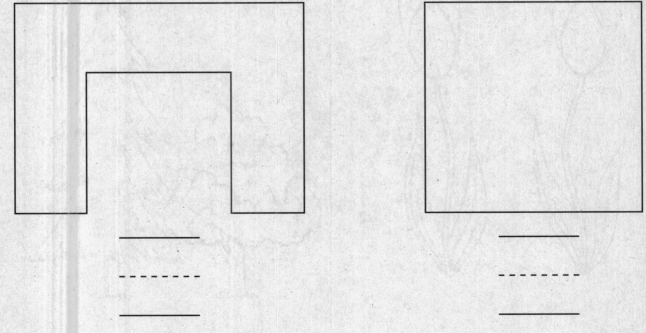

Notes for Home For each pair of shapes, your child guessed which shape could be covered by more Snap Cubes. Then he or she checked each guess using Snap Cubes and recorded the actual number. *Home Activity:* Ask your child to guess how many dimes will fit on one of the shapes and to check his or her guess by putting dimes on the shape.

Compare Lengths

Directions In the top row, color the 2 objects that are the same length blue. In the bottom row, color the objects that are the same height red. **Notes for Home** Your child compared lengths. *Home Activity:* Ask your child to name fruits or vegetables that are about the same length. Then ask your child to compare two vegetables and identify which is longer and which is shorter.

Estimate Length

Directions Color objects about 1 Snap Cube long blue. Color objects about 5 Snap Cubes long red. Color objects about 10 Snap Cubes long yellow. **Notes for Home** Your child estimated the length of objects as either 1 Snap Cube, 5 Snap Cubes, or 10 Snap Cubes long. *Home Activity:* Ask your child to name an object he or she brings to school every day that is about 1 Snap Cube, 5 Snap Cubes, and 10 Snap Cubes long.

Name _____

Use Numbers to Describe Length

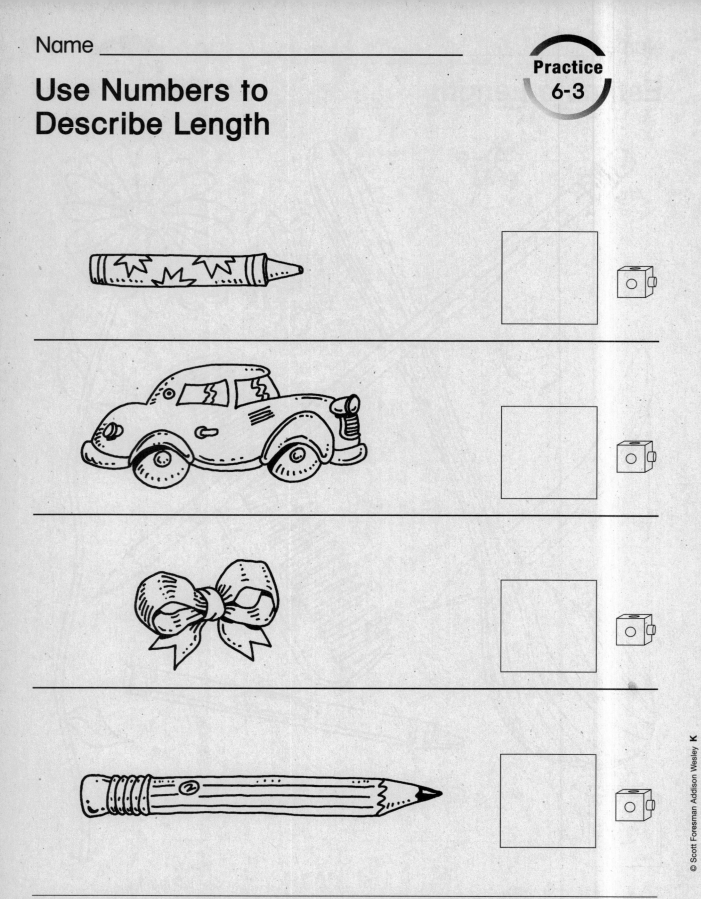

© Scott Foresman Addison Wesley **K**

Directions Use Snap Cubes to measure the object. Then write how many Snap Cubes long each object is in the box. **Notes for Home** Your child used Snap Cubes to measure the length of each object. *Home Activity:* Ask your child to use paper clips to measure the length of his or her hand.

Problem Solving: Use Objects

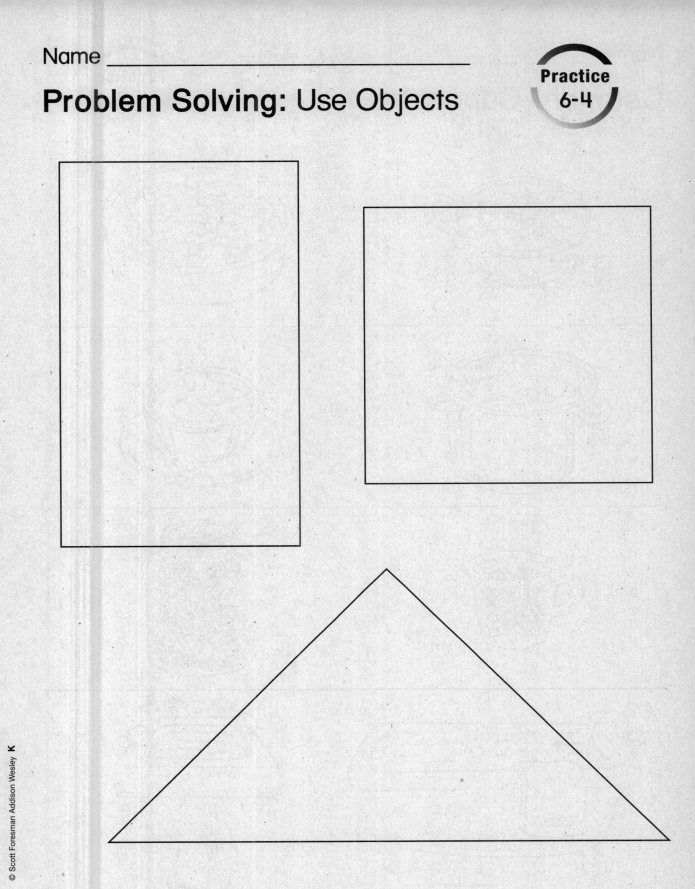

Directions Choose a unit and find the shape that has the longest path around it. Color the shape with the longest path around it. **Notes for Home** Your child used a unit of choice to measure and find the shape with the longest path around it. *Home Activity:* Ask your child to walk around rooms of your house and tell which room has the longest distance around.

Compare Capacities

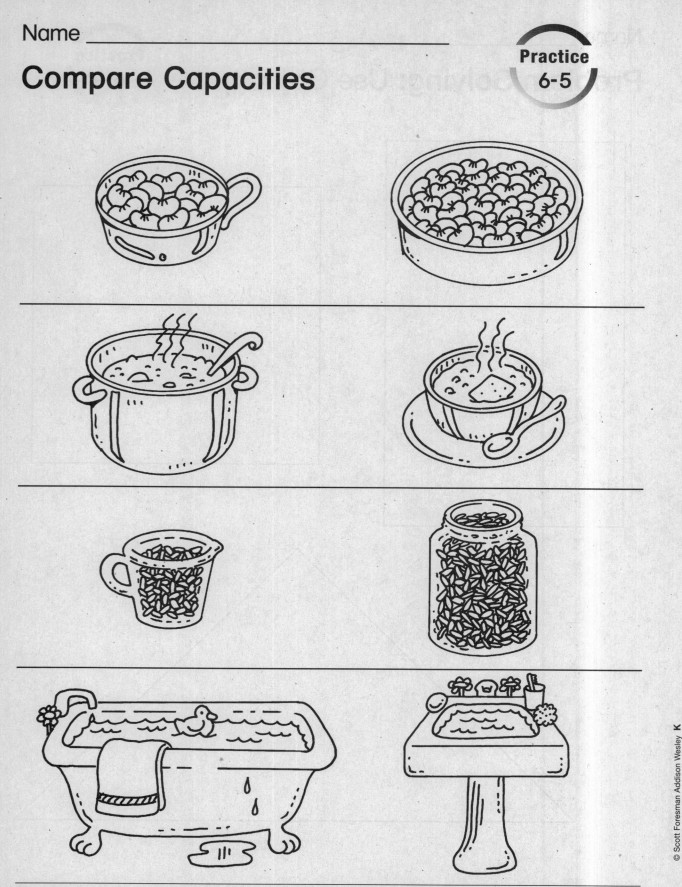

Directions In each row, circle the container that holds more. **Notes for Home** Your child compared sets of containers and identified those that hold more. *Home Activity:* Ask your child to choose two containers in the kitchen and identify which could hold more paper clips. Work together to test the prediction.

Use Numbers to Describe Capacity

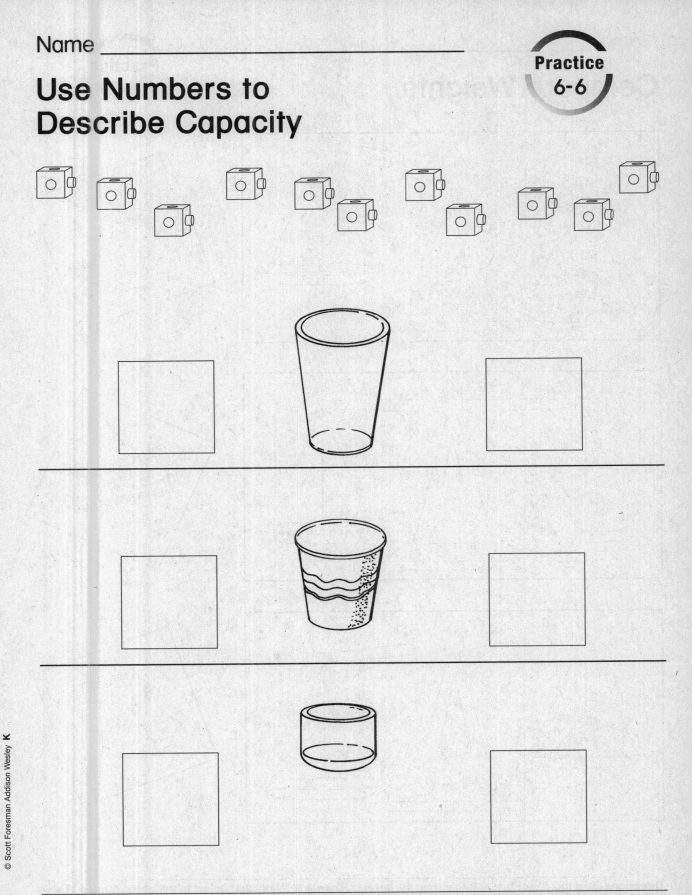

Directions Choose one of the containers: glass, paper cup or plastic food-storage container. Estimate the number of cubes that would fit in the container. Test your estimate. Write the number of cubes that fit. **Notes for Home** Your child estimated and tested the number of cubes that could fill each container. *Home Activity:* Have your child choose two cups or glasses in your home, then tell which holds more.

Compare Weights

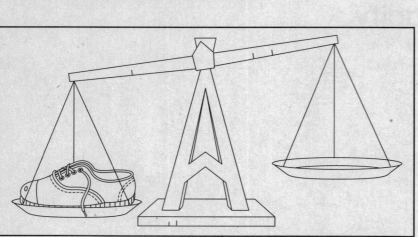

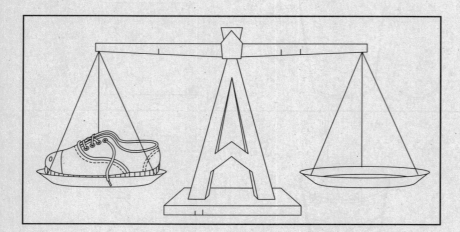

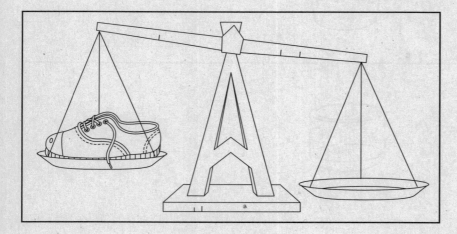

Directions Find the object that is lighter than the sneaker. Draw a line from that object to the pan in the top box. Draw a line from the object that is about the same weight as the sneaker to the pan in the middle box. Draw a line from the object that is heavier than the sneaker to the pan in the bottom box. **Notes for Home** Your child used the terms *heavier, lighter,* and *about the same* to compare weights. *Home Activity:* Have your child show you something heavier, lighter, and about the same weight as a piece of fruit.

Name _____

Estimate Weights

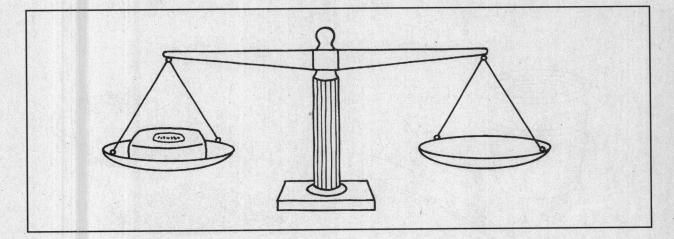

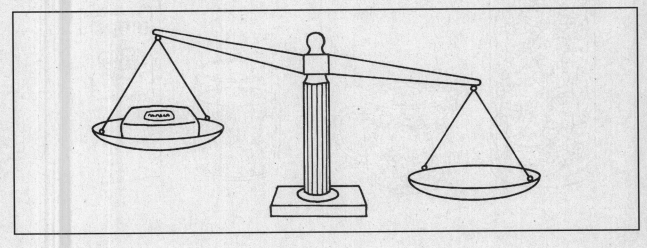

Directions Top Box: Draw something that is about the same weight as the bar of soap. Middle Box: Draw something that is lighter than the bar of soap. Bottom Box: Draw something that is heavier than the bar of soap. **Notes for Home** Your child drew pictures to show objects that are *heavier than, lighter than,* or *weigh about the same as* another object. *Home Activity:* Ask your child to show you objects at home that are heavier, lighter, and about the same weight as a full bar of soap.

Problem Solving: Act it Out

Directions Use containers like the ones on this page. Fill them with the materials shown or substitute other materials that are available. For each pair, circle the container that holds more. **Notes for Home** Your child compared pairs of containers to identify which container holds more. *Home Activity:* Ask your child to show you two containers in your refrigerator or kitchen and to identify which container holds more.

Explore Solids

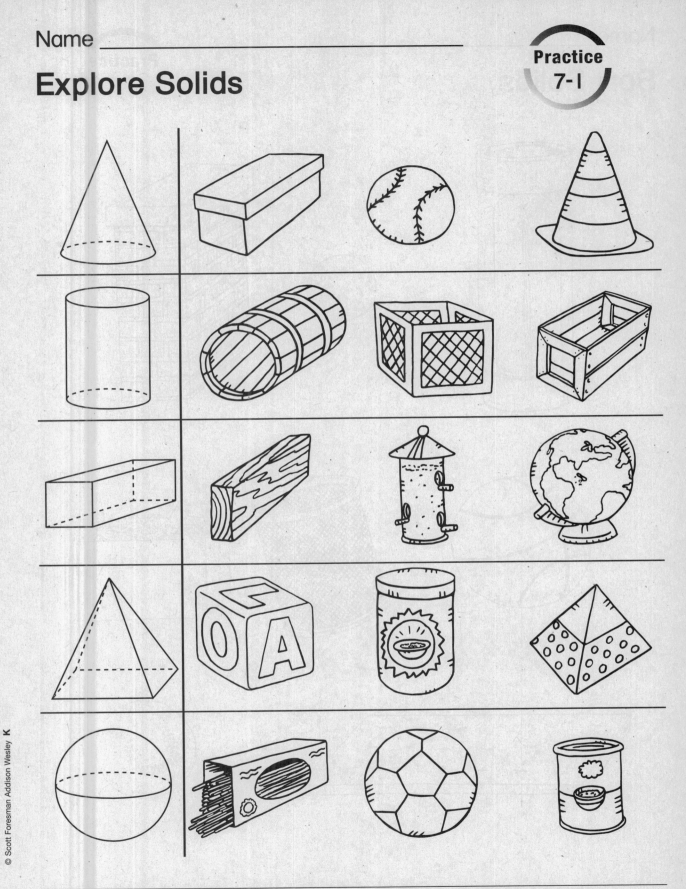

Directions For each row, circle the object on the right that is about the same as the solid on the left.
Notes for Home Your child found objects that were the same shape as boxes, cones, pyramids, cans, and balls.
Home Activity: Ask your child to identify solid shapes found in his or her toys and games at home.

Sort Solids

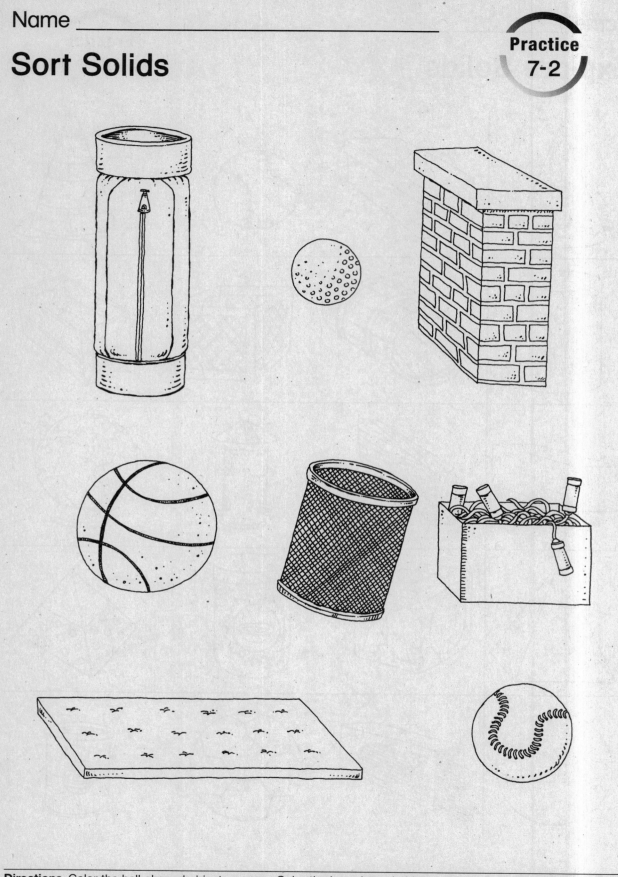

Directions Color the ball-shaped objects orange. Color the box-shaped objects yellow. Color the can-shaped objects blue. **Notes for Home** Your child sorted solids that are box-shaped, can-shaped, and ball-shaped. *Home Activity:* Ask your child to find these same shapes at meal time in foods or tools used for cooking and eating.

Find Shapes in Solids

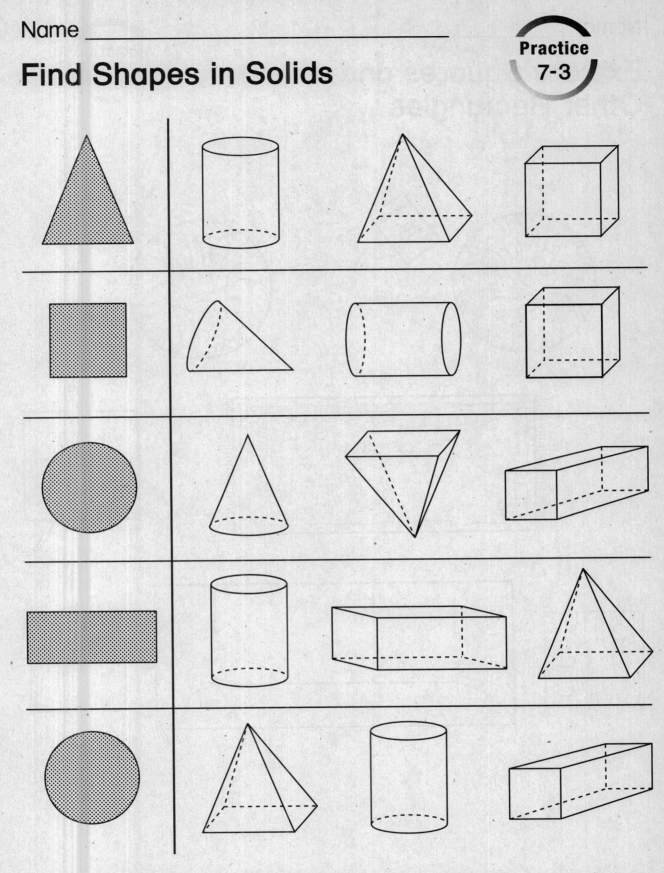

Directions For each row, color the face on each solid shape that matches the shaded stamp print.
Notes for Home Your child found shapes in solids. *Home Activity:* Help your child make a cylinder by cutting out two paper circles the same size for the bottom and top, then cutting out a rectangle to form the cylinder body. Use tape to create the body shape, then attach the bottom and top circles with tape.

Explore Squares and Other Rectangles

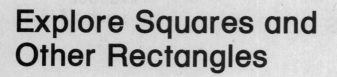

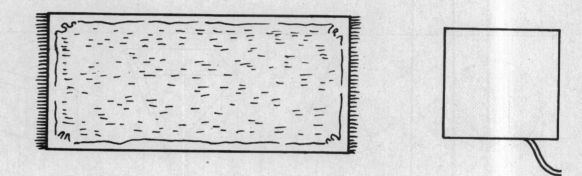
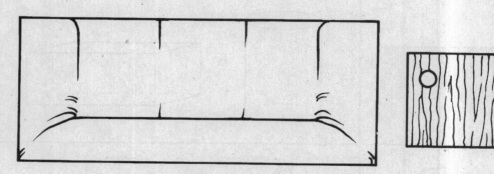

Directions Color the rectangles green. Color the squares red. Color the circles blue. Then draw something else in the living room that is a rectangle or square shape. **Notes for Home** Your child identified and drew rectangles, squares, and circles. *Home Activity:* Ask your child to show you a rectangle and square object in your home, and to compare their sides and corners.

Name _____

Explore Circles and Triangles

Directions Trace the circles you see red. Trace the triangles you see blue. **Notes for Home** Your child identified circles and triangles. *Home Activity:* Help your child trace a circular object onto a sheet of paper.

Name _____

Combine and Separate Shapes

Practice 7-6

© Scott Foresman Addison Wesley K

Directions Look at the picture. What do you see? (a boat) Draw lines to match the shapes that were used to make the boat. **Notes for Home** Your child found shapes in a picture. *Home Activity:* Ask your child to draw a picture of a house made from triangles, squares, and rectangles.

64 Use with pages 165–166.

Problem Solving: Use Objects

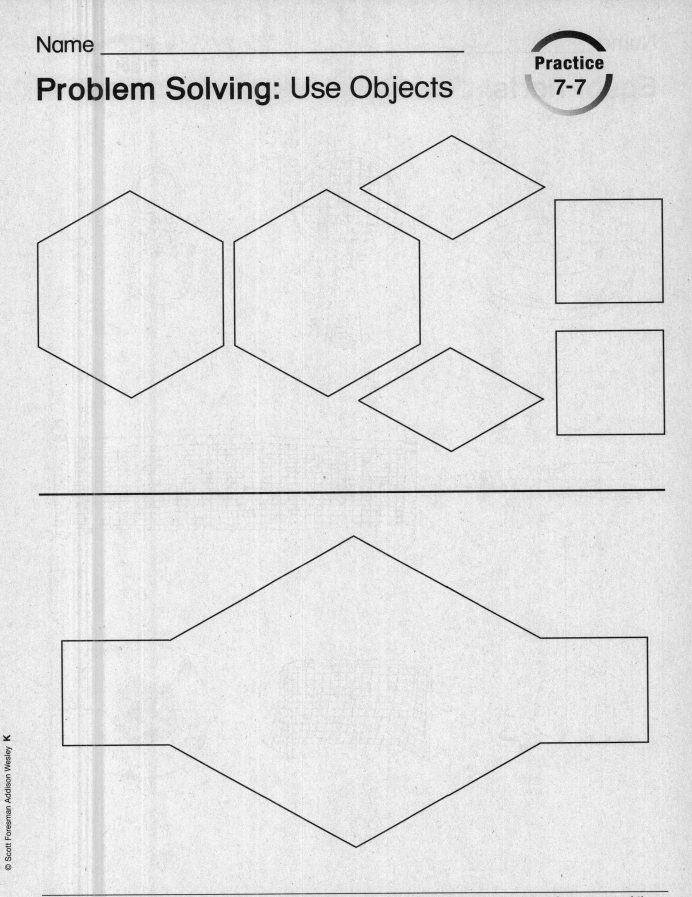

Directions Use the 6 pattern blocks to cover the larger shape. Draw lines and color to show where you used the shapes. **Notes for Home** Your child found shapes in a larger shape. *Home Activity:* Have your child draw a picture of a large shape and show you two or more smaller shapes within it.

Name _____

Equal Parts

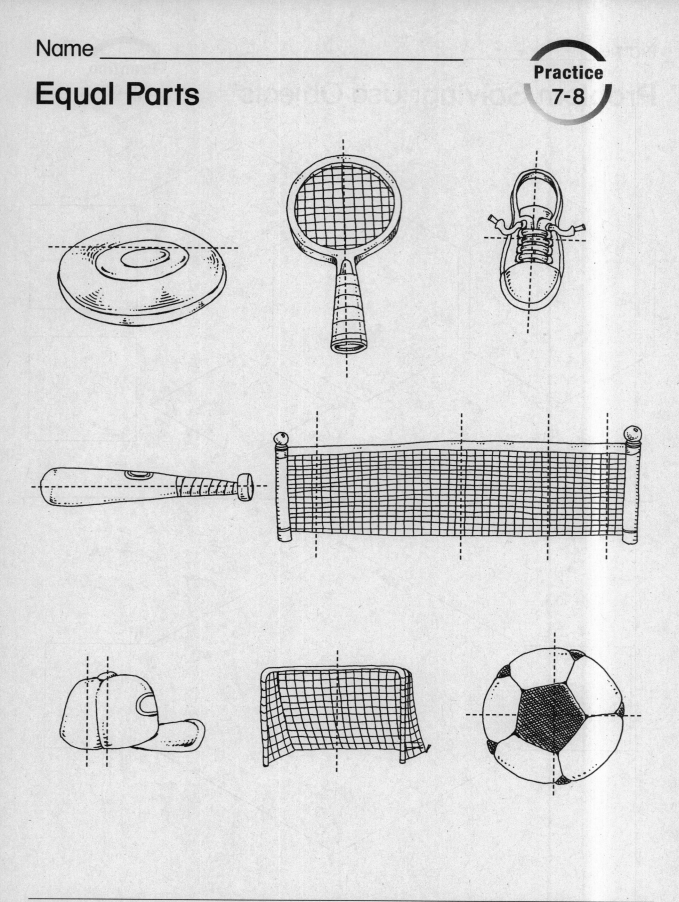

Directions Circle the sports objects that show equal parts. **Notes for Home** Your child identified objects divided into equal parts. *Home Activity:* Have your child show you how a cracker or a piece of bread could be divided into equal parts.

Name _____

Identify Halves

Directions Circle the objects that show halves. **Notes for Home** Your child identified objects separated in halves.
Home Activity: Have your child separate a piece of bread in halves.

Name _____

Make Equal Groups

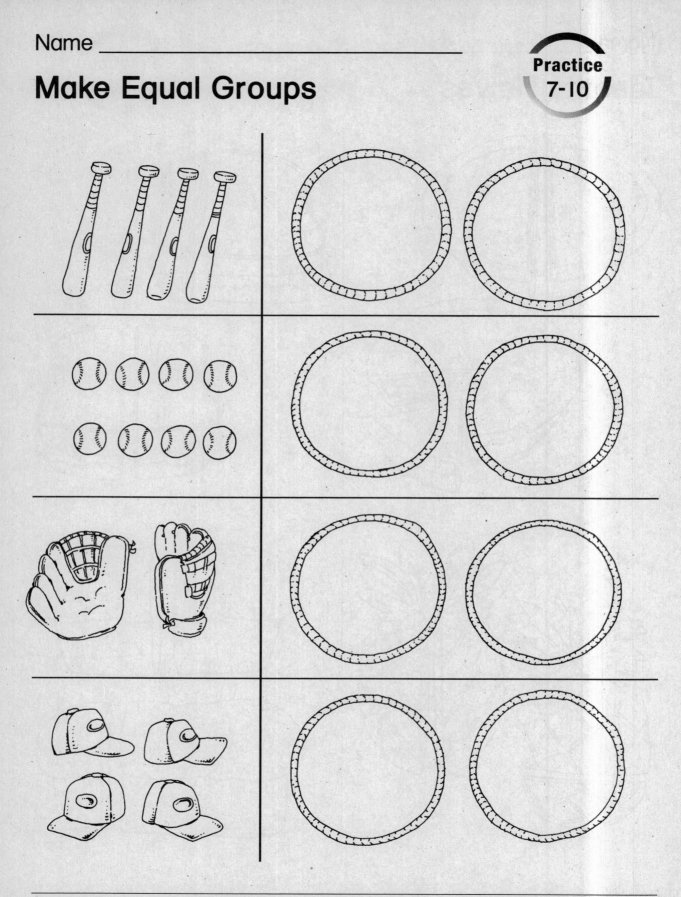

Directions For each row, draw equal groups of the objects in each of the two baskets. **Notes for Home** Your child made equal groups. *Home Activity:* Have your child collect a group of 6 similar objects, such as pencils or crayons. Then have your child make two equal groups of 3 objects.

Problem Solving: Draw a Picture

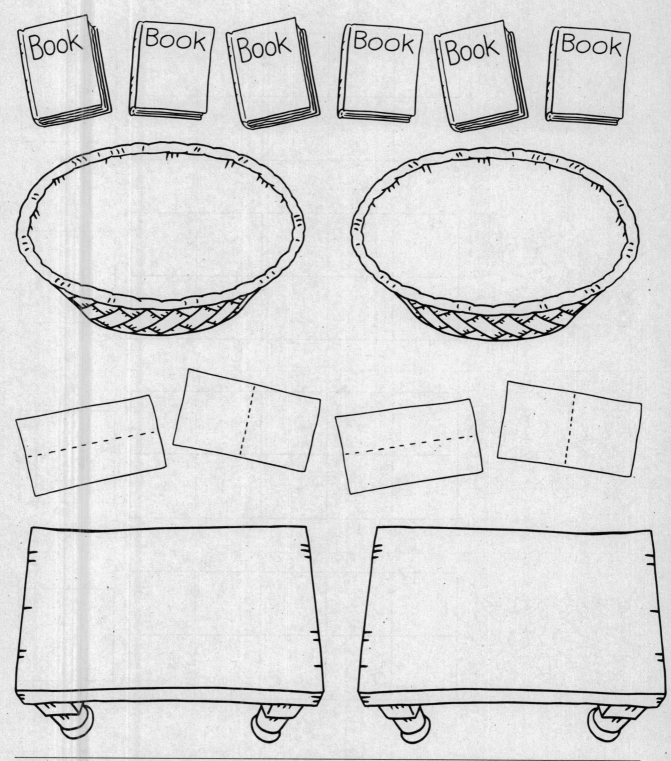

Directions Draw pictures in the baskets to show equal shares of the books. Then half each piece of paper at the dotted line and draw pictures on the table tops to show equal shares of the paper cut in halves. **Notes for Home** Your child drew pictures of equal shares. *Home Activity:* Have your child make equal shares for each of you of a group of magazines, newspapers, or books you have at home.

Name _____

Represent Numbers to 10

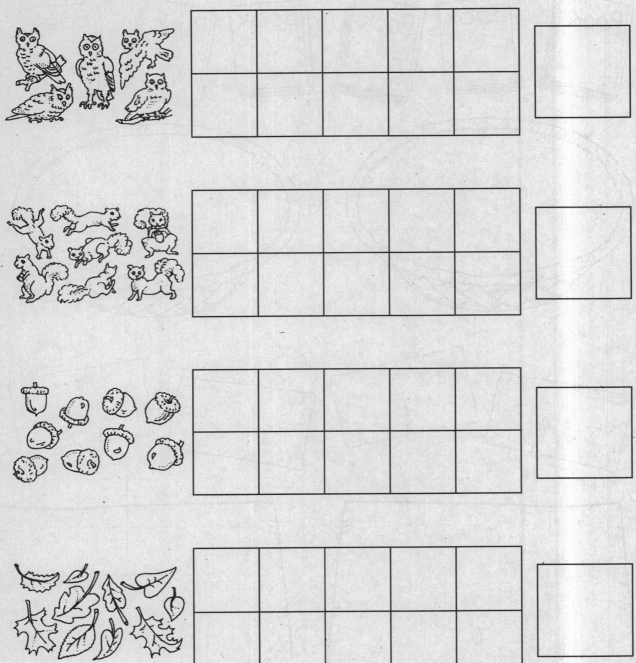

Directions Draw circles in the ten-frame to show the number of animals in each row. Then write the number in the box. **Notes for Home** Your child showed numbers up to 10 in ten-frames. *Home Activity:* Give your child 10 grapes, toothpicks, paper clips, or other small objects. Ask your child to show different ways to make 10.

Name _____

Practice
8-2

Ways to Make 3 and 4

Directions For each box, write X's and O's in each ten-frame to show a different way to make 3 or 4.
Notes for Home Your child showed different ways to make 3 and 4. *Home Activity:* Ask your child to explain his or her answers.

Ways to Make 5 and 6

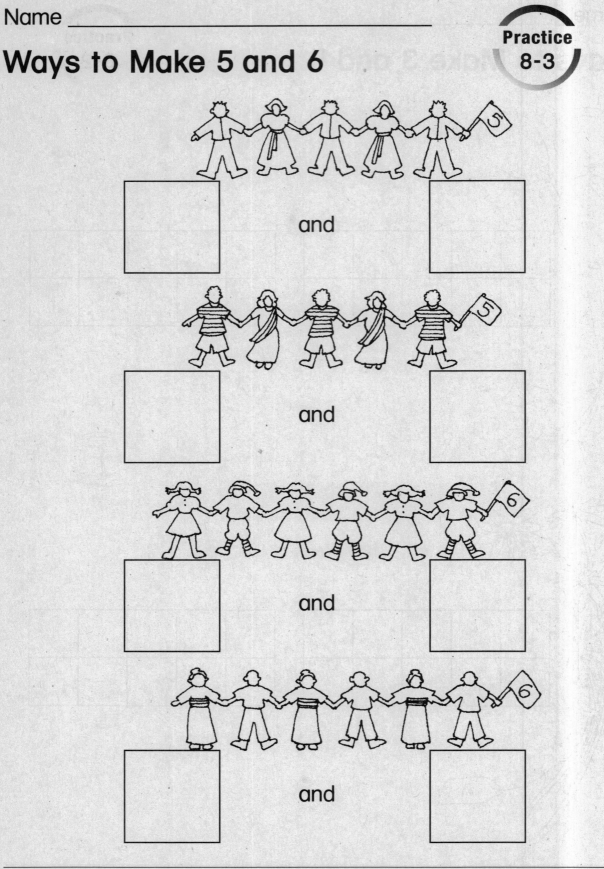

and

and

and

and

Directions Color the first row of paper dolls to show a way to make 5. Color the second row of paper dolls to show another way to make 5. Color the third row of paper dolls to show a way to make 6. Color the fourth row of paper dolls to show a way to make 6. **Notes for Home** Your child showed different ways to make 5 and 6. *Home Activity:* Have your child make 5 using cups and spoons.

Ways to Make 7 and 8

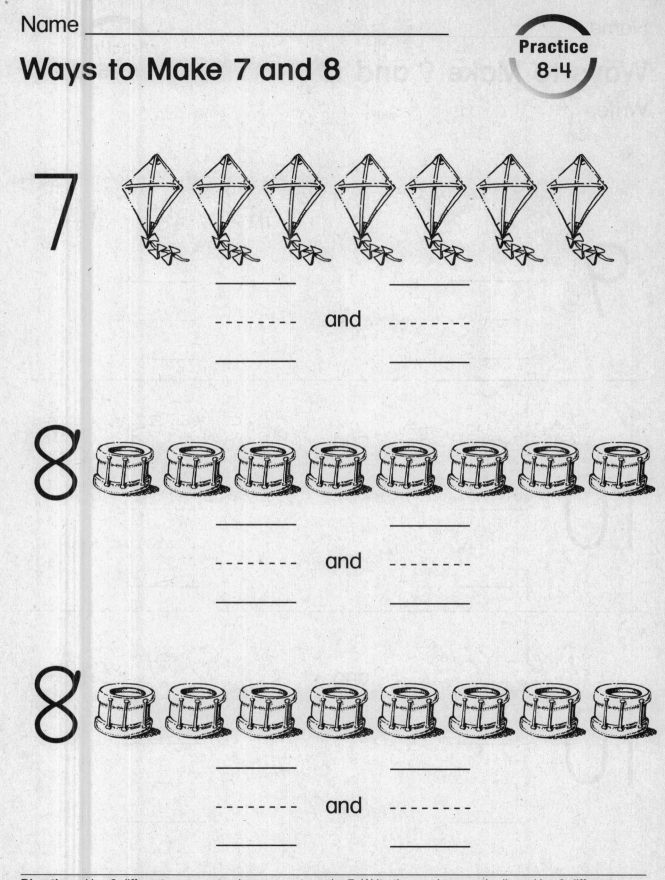

7

_____   and   _____

- - - - - -   and   - - - - - -

_____   and   _____

8

_____   and   _____

- - - - - -   and   - - - - - -

_____   and   _____

8

_____   and   _____

- - - - - -   and   - - - - - -

_____   and   _____

Directions Use 2 different crayons to show a way to make 7. Write the numbers on the lines. Use 2 different crayons to show different ways to make 8. Write the numbers on the lines. **Notes for Home** Your child showed different ways to make 7 and 8. *Home Activity:* Ask your child to clap hands 7 times; then clap 8 times.

Ways to Make 9 and 10

Write.

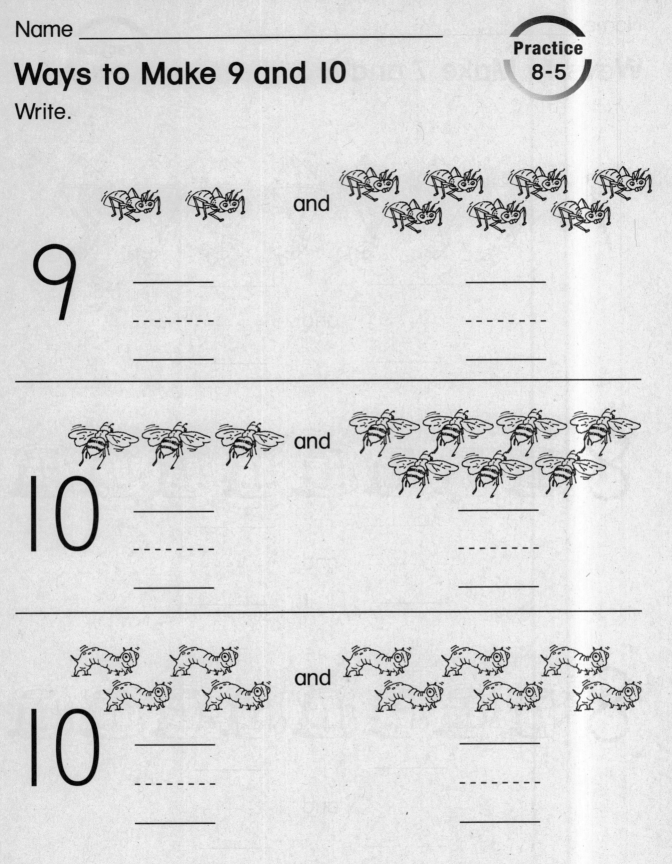

and

9 _____

- - - - - - -

_____

_____

- - - - - - -

_____

and

10 _____

- - - - - - -

_____

_____

- - - - - - -

_____

and

10 _____

- - - - - - -

_____

_____

- - - - - - -

_____

Directions Write the 2 numbers that make 9 ants. Write the 2 numbers that make 10 bees. Write the 2 numbers that make 10 caterpillars. **Notes for Home** Ask your child to tell you another way to make 10 caterpillars and another way to make 9 ants. (Possible answers include: 5 and 5; 3 and 6.)

Problem Solving:
Look for a Pattern

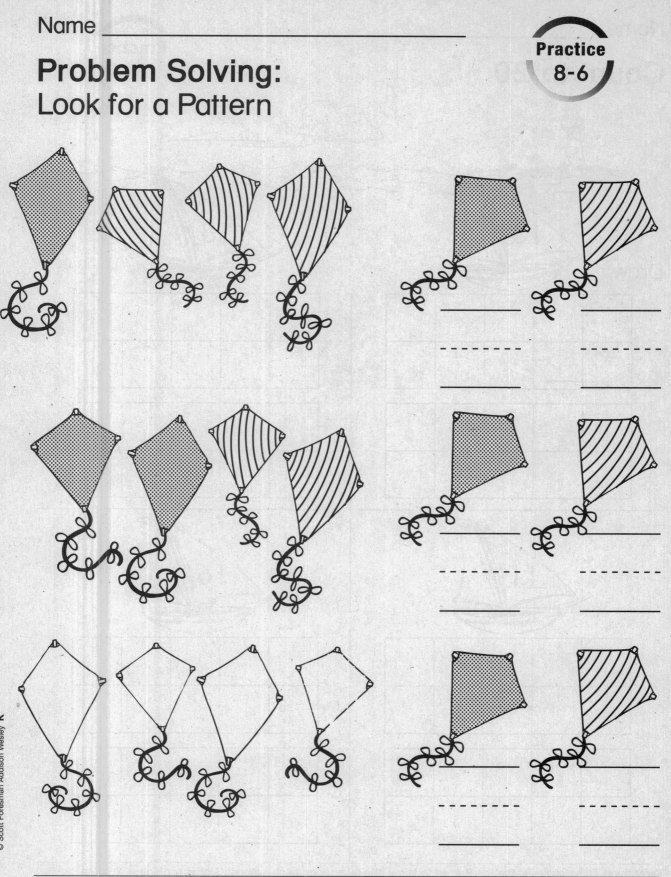

Directions Write the number of shaded kites and the number of striped kites in the top and middle rows. Look for a pattern. Shade or draw stripes on the kites in the bottom row to continue the pattern. **Notes for Home** Your child identified and recorded numbers to describe a pattern. *Home Activity:* Ask your child to describe a pattern that may appear on wallpaper and furnishings in your home.

Count to 20

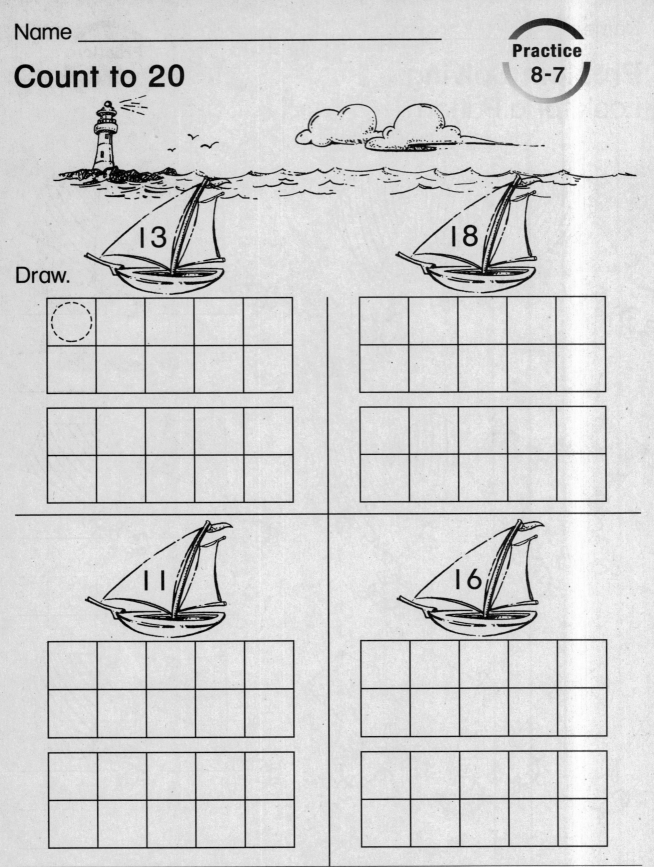

Draw.

Directions Draw circles in the ten-frames to show the number on each sailboat. **Notes for Home** Your child showed numbers up to 20 on ten-frames. *Home Activity:* Have your child count to 20 by pointing to the boxes in 2 ten-frames.

76 Use with pages 195–196.

Name _____

Estimate and Verify Capacity and Weight

Estimate. More than 10.

Fewer than 10.

Measure.

Draw.

Estimate. More than 10.

Fewer than 10.

Measure.

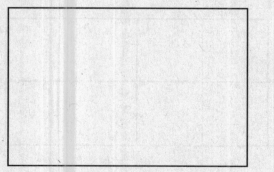

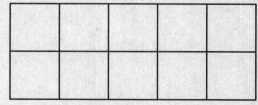

Directions Estimate how many apples it would take to equal the weight of a your math book. Circle the answer. Use a balance scale to check. Then draw circles in the ten-frames to match the number of apples. Find another object that would take fewer than 10 marbles to balance on the scale. Draw it in the box. Draw circles to show the number of marbles on the ten-frame. **Notes for Home** Your child estimated and measured the weight of objects. *Home Activity:* Have your child compare weights of two fruits on a scale in a store.

Name _____

Name _____

Estimate and Verify Length

Directions Choose an object that is longer than 10 Snap Cubes and one object that is shorter than 10 Snap Cubes. Estimate and measure the length of each object. Draw each object. Then color the ten-frame to record the actual number of Snap Cubes used to measure each object. **Notes for Home** Your child estimated and measured the lengths of objects. *Home Activity:* Have your child estimate the length of a table top using straws, then measure it.

78 Use with pages 199–200.

Problem Solving: Draw a Picture

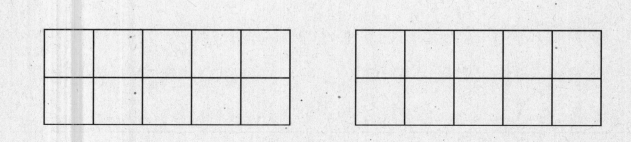

Directions Draw the feet on the girl and the animals. Color the ten-frames to show the number of feet you drew all together. **Notes for Home** Your child drew a picture to solve a problem. *Home Activity:* Have your child draw himself or herself and 2 friends; then write how many feet there are. (6)

Discuss Before and After

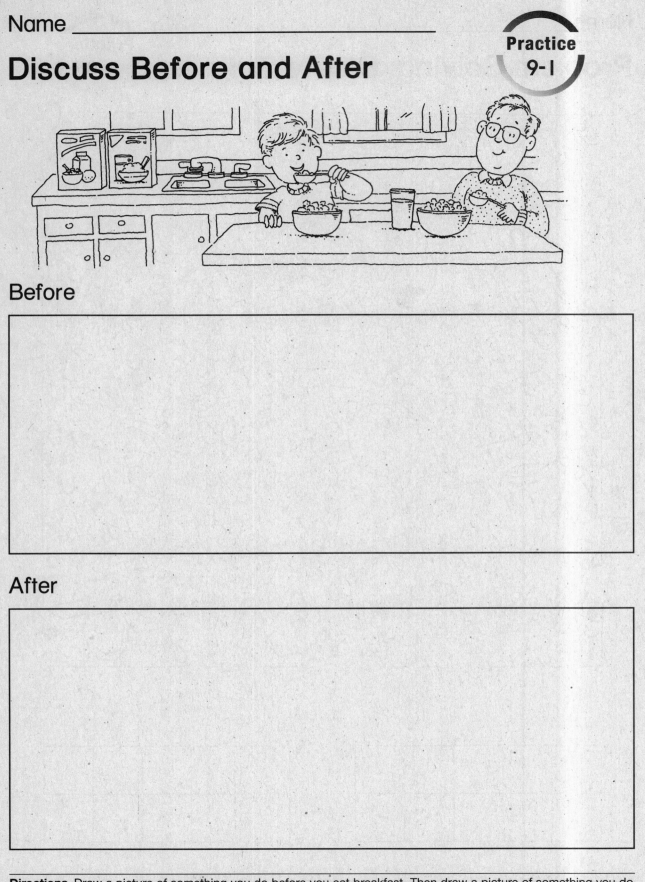

Before

After

Directions Draw a picture of something you do before you eat breakfast. Then draw a picture of something you do after you eat breakfast. **Notes for Home** Your child drew pictures to show what he or she does before eating breakfast and after breakfast. *Home Activity:* Ask your child to discuss something done before lunch and something done after lunch on a day when there is no school.

Directions For each row of pictures, write 1, 2, or 3 to show which happens first, next, and last.

Notes for Home Your child ordered events by describing what happened first, next, and last. *Home Activity:* Ask your child to describe how he or she gets a drink from the refrigerator or faucet using the words *first, next,* and *last.*

Locate Numbers on a Clock

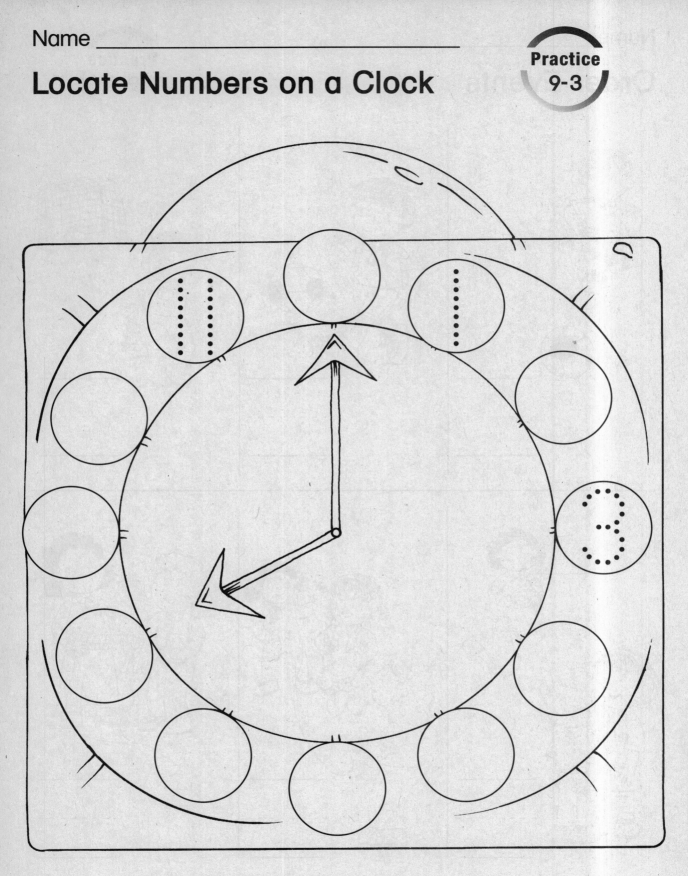

Directions Write the numbers on the clock. **Notes for Home** Your child wrote numbers on a clock. *Home Activity:* Show your child a clock or watch. Ask your child to point to numbers 3, 5, 8, and 12 on the clock or watchface.

Tell Time to the Hour

☐:00

_____
- - - - - - -
_____ o'clock

☐:00

_____
- - - - - - -
_____ o'clock

☐:00

_____
- - - - - - -
_____ o'clock

☐:00

_____
- - - - - - -
_____ o'clock

☐:00

_____
- - - - - - -
_____ o'clock

☐:00

_____
- - - - - - -
_____ o'clock

Directions Write the time to the hour shown on each clockface two other ways. **Notes for Home** Your child wrote time to the hour shown on a clock in two different ways. *Home Activity:* Ask your child where the hour and minute hands are on the clock when it is 12 o'clock. (Both point to 12.)

Problem Solving: Make a Picture

At the Water

Directions Draw pictures of things you do to get ready to play on a beach, at a pool, a lake, or a pond.
Notes for Home Your child drew pictures about an activity. *Home Activity:* Ask your child to describe how he or she gets ready to go to bed. Then have your child draw pictures to show what he or she does.

Use Pennies and Nickels

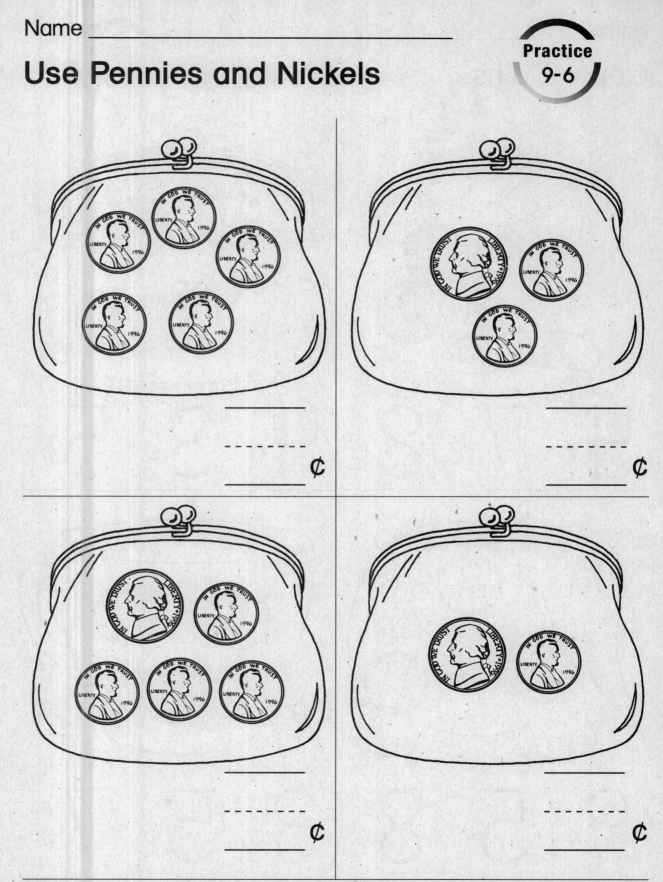

_ _ _ _ _ _ _ _
¢

_ _ _ _ _ _ _ _
¢

_ _ _ _ _ _ _ _
¢

_ _ _ _ _ _ _ _
¢

Directions Write a number in each box to show how many cents are in each purse. **Notes for Home** Your child counted coins to 9¢ and wrote the number to tell how many cents. *Home Activity:* Ask your child to show you two ways to show 5¢. (5 pennies or 1 nickel)

Count Coins

4 ¢   7 ¢   (8) ¢   4 ¢   3 ¢   5 ¢

9 ¢   5 ¢   8 ¢   3 ¢   5 ¢   7 ¢

Directions Circle the total amount of money shown in each picture. **Notes for Home** Your child counted coins to 9¢. *Home Activity:* Ask your child to show you two ways to show 6¢ with nickels and pennies. (6 pennies or 1 penny and 1 nickel)

Name _____

Use Dimes

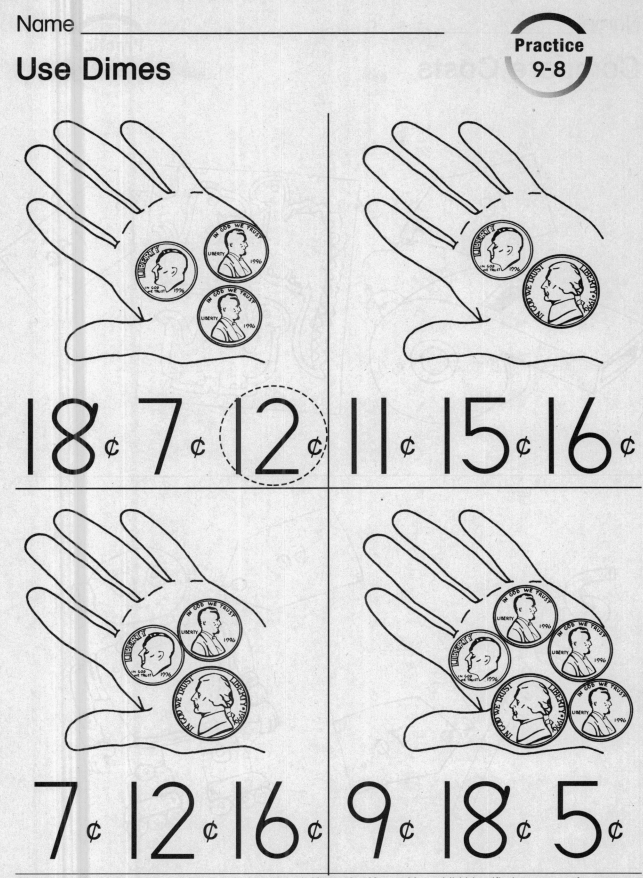

18¢   7¢   (12¢) | 11¢   15¢   16¢

7¢   12¢   16¢ | 9¢   18¢   5¢

Directions Circle the amount of money in each hand. **Notes for Home** Your child identified amounts of money to 19¢ shown with dimes, nickels, and pennies. *Home Activity:* Make available a quantity of pennies, nickels, and dimes. Ask your child to show you 17¢ with at least two kinds of coins. (Possible answers: 1 nickel, 12 pennies; 2 nickels, 7 pennies; 1 dime, 7 pennies; 1 dime, 1 nickel, 2 pennies)

Name _____

Compare Costs

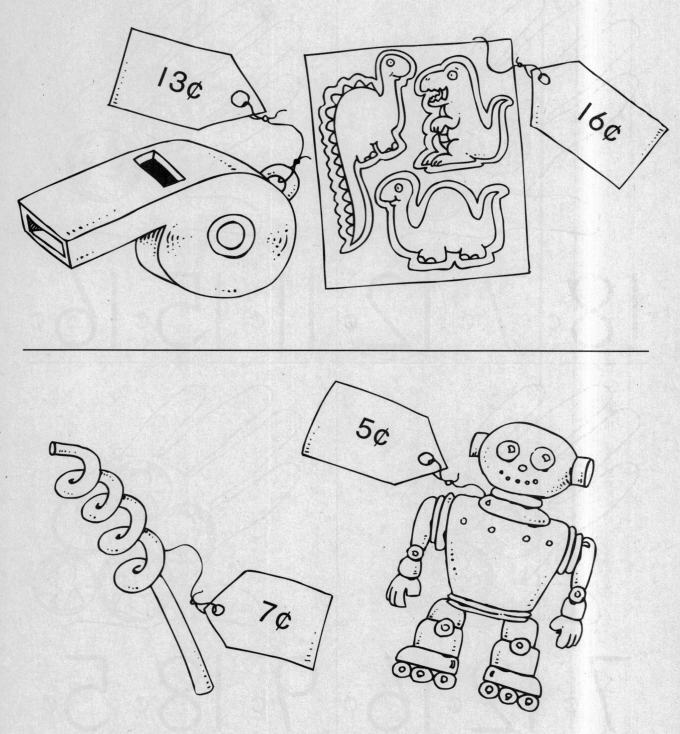

13¢

16¢

5¢

7¢

Directions For each row, color the object that costs more blue, and color the object that costs less red.
Notes for Home Your child compared costs. *Home Activity:* Look at prices in a newspaper advertisement. Ask your child to compare two prices by telling which is more and which is less.

Problem Solving: Act It Out

Directions Color one or more objects you could buy at the sale with 16¢. **Notes for Home** Your child determined objects that could be bought for 16¢. *Home Activity:* Ask your child what he or she would buy with 12¢.

Explore Joining

Directions Look at the picture. Listen to this story. *2 children are on the school bus. 3 more children get on the school bus. Tell how many children are on the school bus now.* Use your Snap Cubes to act out the story.
Notes for Home Your child listened to a joining story and found how many in all. *Home Activity:* Ask your child to tell you a joining story about the picture on this page.

Join Groups

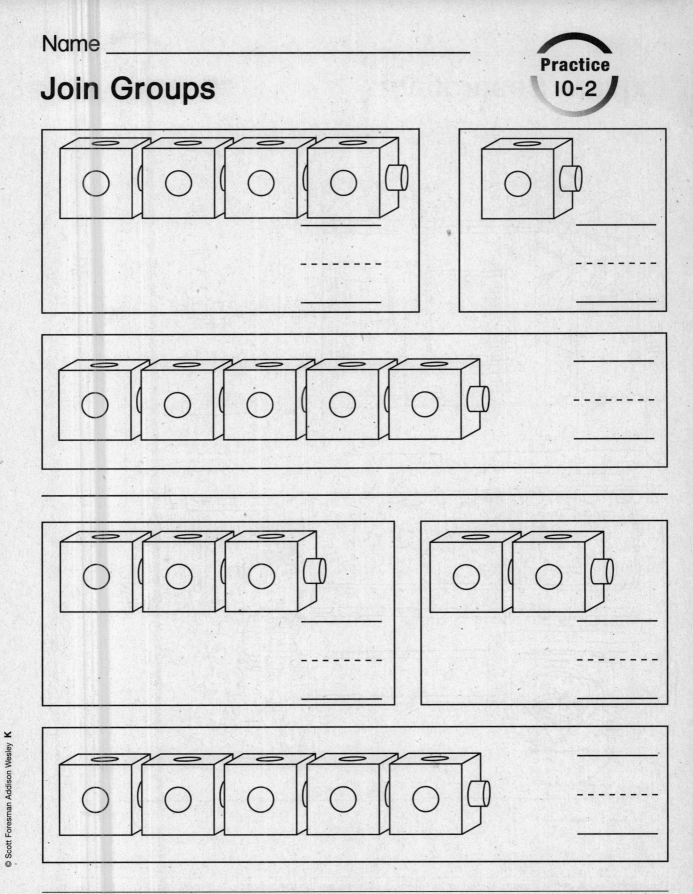

Directions At the top, count the Snap Cubes in the left box. Write how many. Count the Snap Cubes in the right box. Write how many. Count the Snap Cubes in the long box. Write how many in all. Do the same for the bottom boxes. **Notes for Home** Your child counted and joined groups to tell how many in all. *Home Activity:* Ask your child to make up a joining story about one group of boxes.

Explore Separating

Directions Look at the picture. Listen to the story. *5 children are on the school bus. 2 children get off the bus. How many children are still left on the bus?* Use your Snap Cubes to act out the story. **Notes for Home** Your child listened to a separating story and found how many were left. *Home Activity:* Ask your child to use small objects, such as buttons, to model a story about separating groups.

Name _____

Separate Groups and Lengths

_____

- - - - - - - - -

_____

are left.

_____

- - - - - - - - -

_____

are left.

Directions Listen to the story for the top picture. *There are 6 boxes on the truck. Workers take 3 boxes off the truck. How many boxes are left on the truck?* Cross out the boxes that were taken away. Write how many are left. Listen to the story for the bottom picture. *There are 6 boxes on the truck. Workers take 2 boxes off the truck. How many boxes are left on the truck?* **Notes for Home** Your child listened to separating stories and wrote how many were left. *Home Activity:* Ask your child to tell you a story about separating groups.

Problem Solving: Act It Out

Directions Look at the top picture and listen to the story. *5 children are playing on the merry-go-round. 1 child gets off the merry-go-round.* How many children are left on the merry-go-round? Look at the bottom picture and listen to the story. *2 children are in the sandbox. 3 more children get in the sandbox.* How many children are in the sandbox in all? Write the number. **Notes for Home** Your child listened to a story about each picture and then wrote the number to answer the question *How many . .?* **Home Activity:** Have family members pretend to be guests. Ask your child to welcome them to the table by telling a story about joining groups.

Explore Comparing

_____
- - - - - - - -
_____ more

_____
- - - - - - - -
_____ fewer

Directions Count the whales in the top picture. Draw another group of whales that shows more. Write how many more. In the bottom picture, count the starfish. Draw another group of starfish that shows fewer. Write how many fewer. **Notes for Home** Your child drew pictures to show more and fewer and wrote numbers. *Home Activity:* Have your child explain his or her drawings using the words *more* and *fewer.*

Compare Groups and Lengths

Compare. Color. Write.

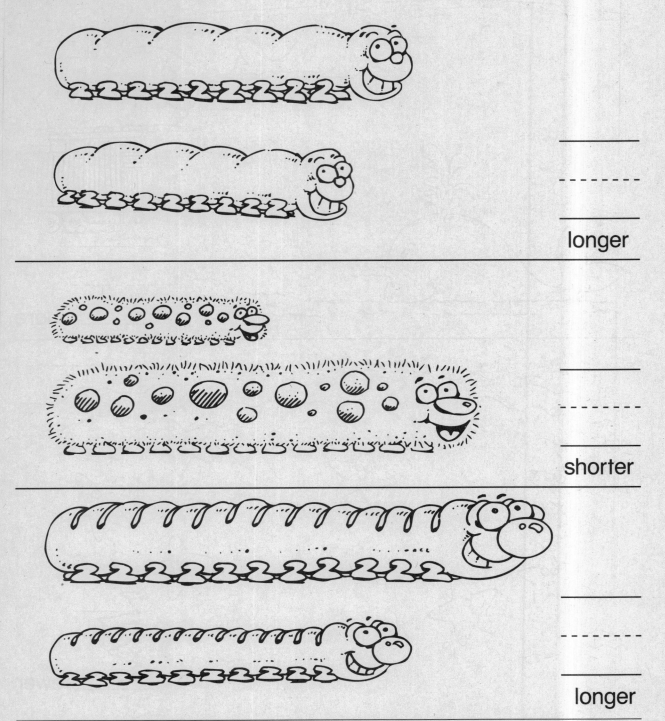

_____

- - - - - -

_____

longer

_____

- - - - - -

shorter

_____

- - - - - -

longer

Directions Look at the caterpillars in the first row. Color the longer one. Then use your Snap Cubes to find how much longer it is than the shorter caterpillar. Write the number in the box. Look at the middle row. How many Snap Cubes shorter is the shorter caterpillar? Look at the bottom row. How many Snap Cubes longer is the longer caterpillar? **Notes for Home** Your child compared the lengths of each pair of caterpillars and wrote a number to tell how many Snap Cubes longer or shorter. *Home Activity:* Ask your child to compare the length of a teaspoon and a fork, and tell which is longer.

Name _____

Problem Solving:
Use Logical Reasoning

Directions Listen to the clues for the pictures in the top row. Which is my train? My train is not the shortest. My train has stripes. Put an X on my train. Point to the bottom box. Which is my lizard? My lizard has no spots. My lizard rests on a tree limb. Circle my lizard. **Notes for Home** Your child listened to clues and used logical reasoning to identify each answer. *Home Activity:* Ask your child to put an X on the train that is the shortest.

Explore Numbers to 31

Draw  .

Notes for Home Your child drew any number of hats to 31 on the shelves and colored that many in the ten-frames. Then your child told how many by describing tens and ones. *Home Activity:* Ask your child to put 23 pieces of pasta into plastic bags as tens and extras.

Name _____

Count and Write 11 to 15

Draw ○. Write.

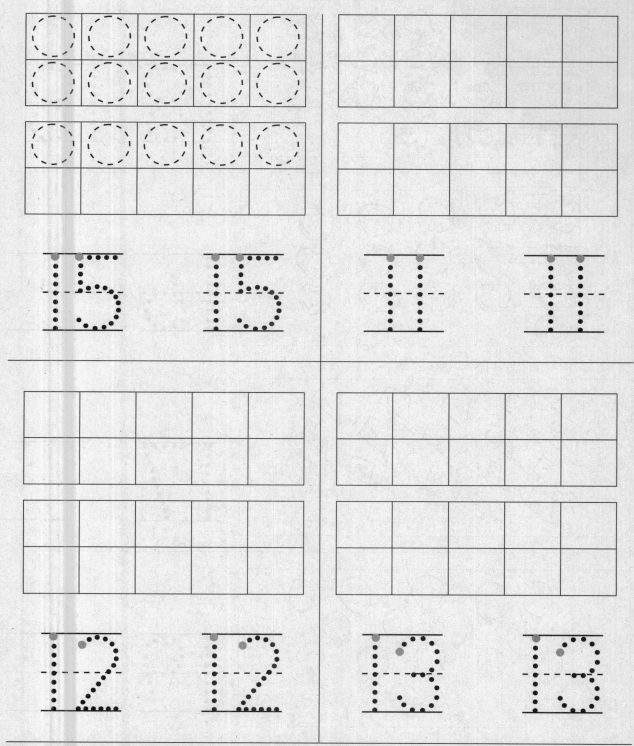

Notes for Home Your child drew circles in the ten-frames and wrote the numbers. *Home Activity:* Have your child count the circles in each box.

Name _____

Count and Write 16 to 19

Circle 10. Count and write.

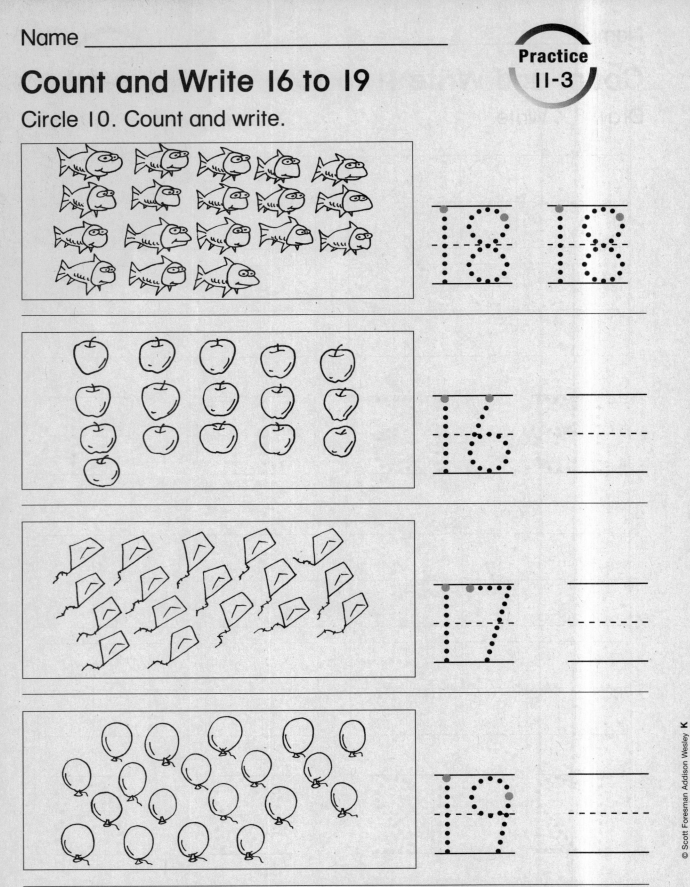

© Scott Foresman Addison Wesley K

Notes for Home Your child counted and wrote the numbers 16 through 19. *Home Activity:* Ask your child to count aloud each box of items.

Name _____

Problem Solving: Use Objects

Write.

Estimate.

[ ]

Count.

[ ]

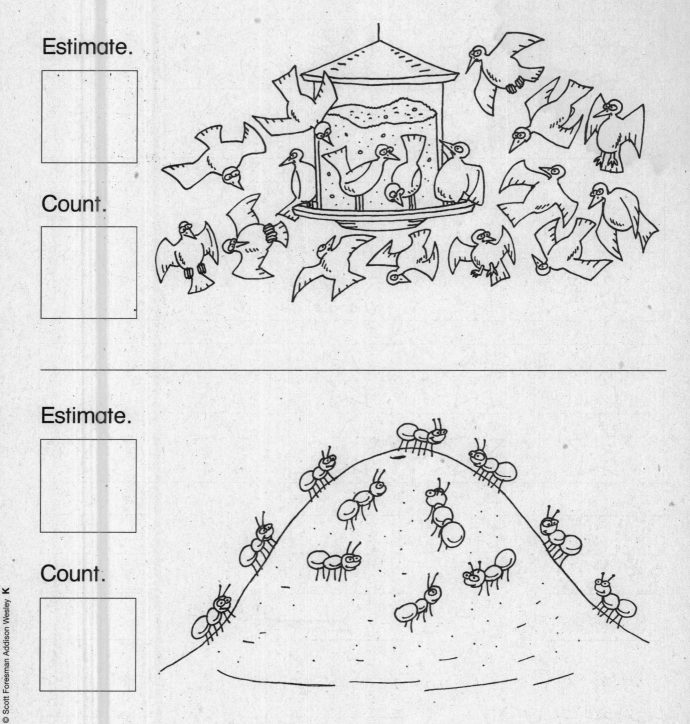

Estimate.

[ ]

Count.

[ ]

Directions About how many birds (ants) do you see? Write your estimate. Place a bean on each bird (ant), and then count the beans. **Notes for Home** Your child estimated and then counted to check the number of animals in each picture. He or she wrote the number to tell how many. *Home Activity:* Ask your child to estimate and check the number of windows in a house or apartment building.

Count and Write Larger Numbers

Count. Write.

Directions Color 25 stars yellow. Write 25. Color the next star. Write how many stars are colored now. Color another star and write how many. Continue coloring and writing until all the stars are colored. **Notes for Home** Your child counted and wrote the numbers 25 through 30. *Home Activity:* Ask your child to count 29 objects.

Name _____

Use a Calendar
Write. Draw.

March

Sunday	Monday	Tuesday	Wednesday	Thursday	Friday	Saturday
		1			4	
6			9			
	14	15				
				24		26
		30				

Notes for Home Your child wrote the numbers 1-31 on the calendar and drew a March scene at the top of the calendar. *Home Activity:* Ask your child to circle the weekends and any other non-school days in March.

© Scott Foresman Addison Wesley **K**

Compare Larger Numbers

Color the group that has fewer.

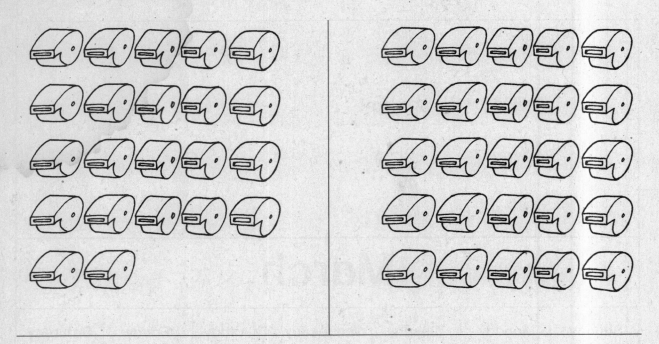

Color the group that has more.

Notes for Home Your child compared groups and colored those with fewer items and those with more items. *Home Activity:* Have your child take two handfuls of pasta—one with the right hand and the other with the left hand. Ask him or her to compare the number of pieces taken and tell which hand has more.

Name _____

Use Larger Numbers for Measurement

Write.

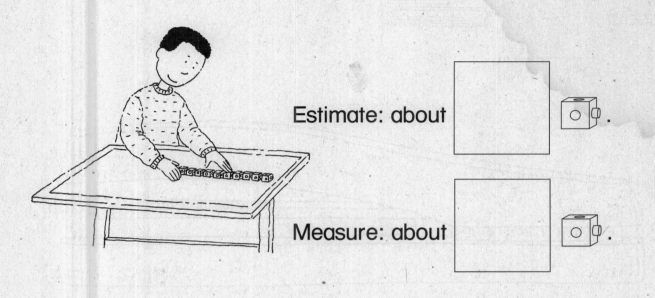

Estimate: about ☐  .

Measure: about ☐ 📦 .

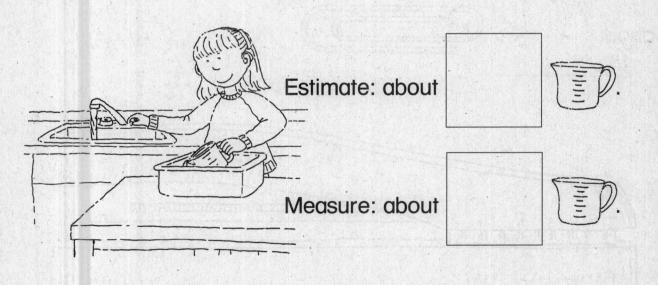

Estimate: about ☐ 🥤 .

Measure: about ☐ 🥤 .

Notes for Home Your child estimated and measured the length of a flannelboard with Snap Cubes. Your child estimated and measured the capacity of a tub with a measuring cup. *Home Activity:* Give your child a measuring cup and a bowl. Ask your child to estimate and measure how many cups of water it would take to fill the bowl.

Problem Solving: Use Objects

Write.

about [ ] 🖇

about [ ]

Sums to 5

© Scott Foresman Addison Wesley K

Directions: Listen to the stories. *4 puppies are with their mother. 1 more puppy comes to join them.* Color to show how many puppies there are in all. Write how many puppies in all. *2 kittens are with their mother. 2 more kittens join them.* Color to show how many in all. Write the number. **Notes for Home** Your child colored counters to show joining stories and wrote the numbers that tell how many in all. *Home Activity:* Have your child tell you a joining story about each picture.

Use with pages 281–282. **107**

Sums to 6 and 7

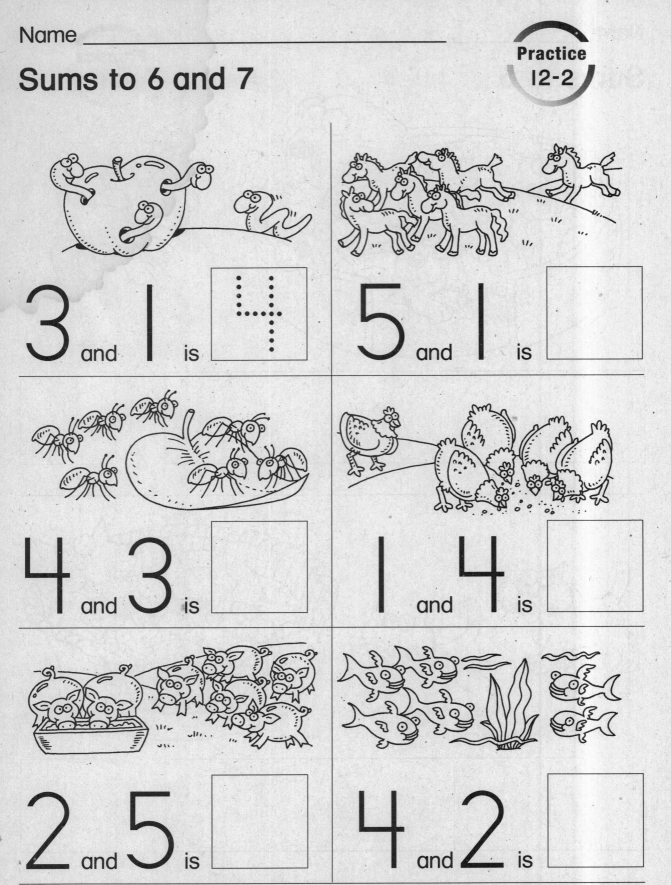

3 and 1 is [4]

5 and 1 is [ ]

4 and 3 is [ ]

1 and 4 is [ ]

2 and 5 is [ ]

4 and 2 is [ ]

Notes for Home Your child wrote the sums for the joining actions. *Home Activity:* Ask your child to use toys to act out adding 1 and then 2 to 5.

Sums to 8 and 9

Use ⬭. Write.

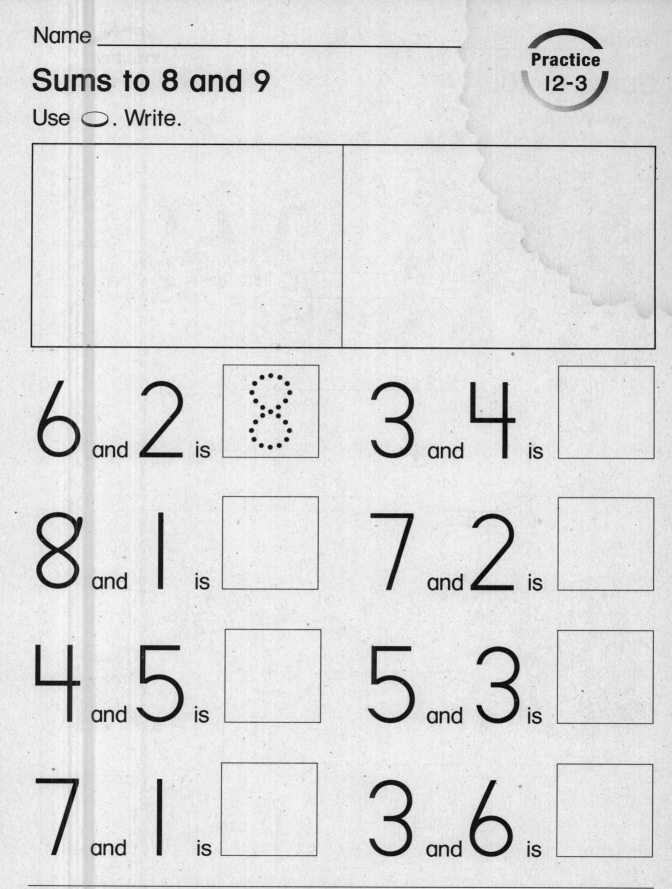

6 and 2 is [8]   3 and 4 is [ ]

8 and 1 is [ ]   7 and 2 is [ ]

4 and 5 is [ ]   5 and 3 is [ ]

7 and 1 is [ ]   3 and 6 is [ ]

Notes for Home Your child used counters to join the groups, then wrote the sums. *Home Activity:* Ask your child to show 7 and 2 with pennies and to tell you the sum.

Sums to 10

Draw. Write.

$\boxed{}$ + $\boxed{}$ = $\boxed{}$

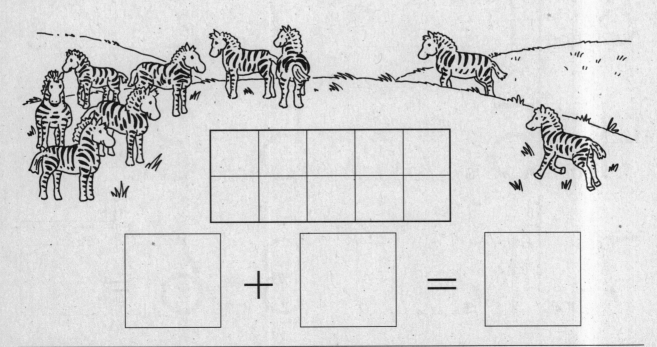

$\boxed{}$ + $\boxed{}$ = $\boxed{}$

© Scott Foresman Addison Wesley **K**

Notes for Home Your child drew circles to show how many animals are in the picture and then wrote the numbers to tell about the picture. *Home Activity:* Ask your child to tell a joining story about one of the pictures.

Name _____

Problem Solving: Act It Out

Use ▢ to act out. Write.

4 + 1 = 5

Directions Make up a story about each picture. Use Snap Cubes to act it out. Then write the numbers and the sum. **Notes for Home** Your child used Snap Cubes to act out a story for each picture and then recorded the addition sentence. *Home Activity:* Ask your child to act out a story about one of the pictures on this page.

Subtract from 5 or Less

_____

- - - - - - - -

_____

_____

- - - - - - - -

_____

Directions Listen to the stories. *5 swans are swimming in a pond. 2 fly away.* Cross out the swans that flew away. Tell how many are left. *5 swans are swimming in a pond. 4 fly away.* **Notes for Home** Your child subtracted from 5. *Home Activity:* Give your child 4 dimes. Take away 1, and ask your child how many are left.

Subtract from 6 and 7

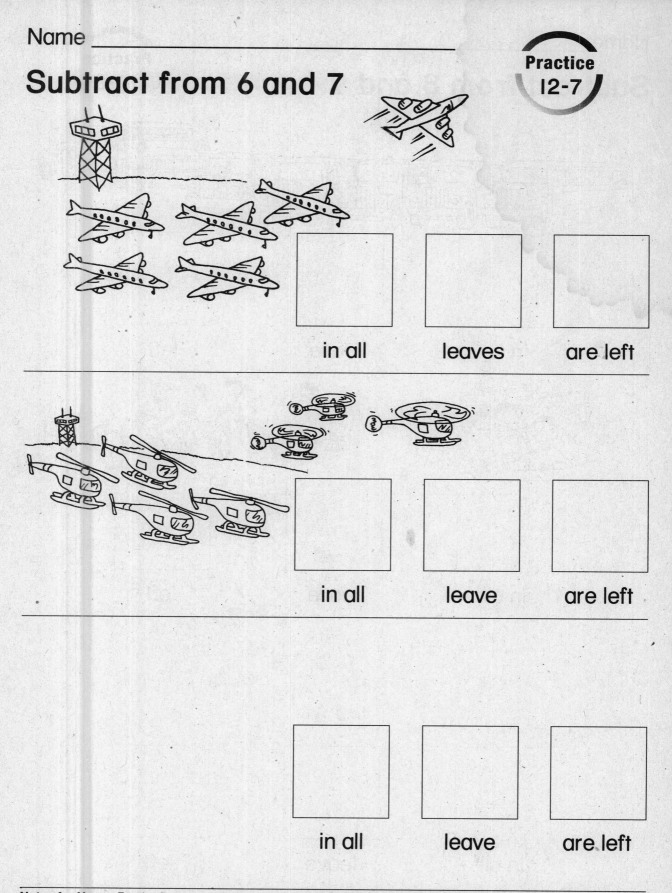

in all   leaves   are left

in all   leave   are left

in all   leave   are left

Notes for Home For the first two exercises, your child told subtraction stories and wrote numbers to tell the stories. For the last exercise, your child drew pictures to match the story that he or she made up. *Home Activity:* Draw squares and cross out 4. Ask your child to tell a story that matches the picture.

Subtract from 8 and 9

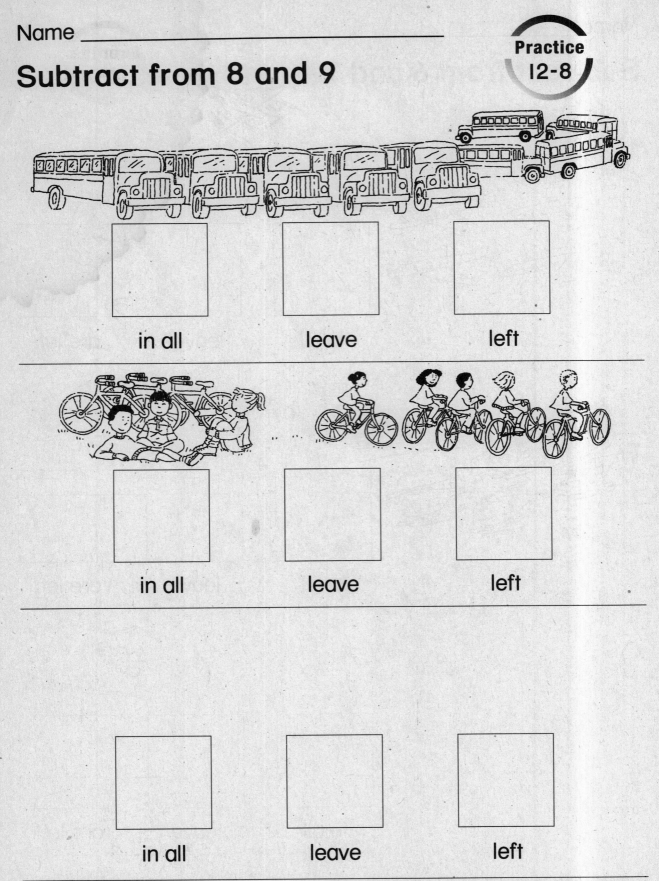

in all   leave   left

in all   leave   left

in all   leave   left

Notes for Home For the first two exercises, your child told subtraction stories and wrote numbers to tell the stories. For the last exercise, your child drew pictures to match the story that he or she made up. *Home Activity:* Ask your child to tell you a story about the picture he or she drew in the last row.

Subtract from 10

Write.

10 – 2 = ____

9 – 4 = ____

9 – 2 = ____

10 – 3 = ____

Notes for Home Ask your child to tell a subtraction story for each picture and to write the number that tells how many are left. *Home Activity:* Ask your child to show you 10 pennies, give some to another person, and tell a number story that includes how many are left.

Problem Solving:
Choose the Operation

Listen. Circle. Write.

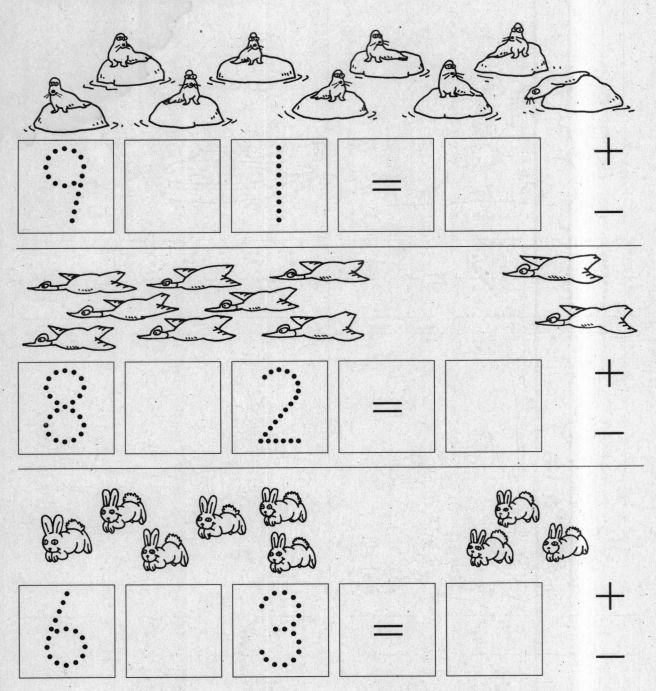

Directions Listen to each story. Decide if you should add or subtract. Circle the correct sign. Then complete the number sentence. *9 seals are sunbathing on the rocks. 1 swims away. How many are left? 8 geese are flying together. 2 more geese join them. How many geese in all? 6 rabbits are hopping toward the woods. 3 more rabbits join them. How many rabbits in all?* **Notes for Home** Your child listened to stories, chose whether to add or subtract, and solved the problem. Ask your child to explain his or her choices.